Taking Action

Taking Action

REINHARD
BONNKE,DD

CHARISMA
HOUSE

Most Charisma House Book Group products are available at special quantity discounts for bulk purchase for sales promotions, premiums, fund-raising, and educational needs. For details, write Charisma House Book Group, 600 Rinehart Road, Lake Mary, Florida 32746, or telephone (407) 333-0600.

Taking Action by Reinhard Bonnke
Published by Charisma House
Charisma Media/Charisma House Book Group
600 Rinehart Road
Lake Mary, Florida 32746
www.charismahouse.com

Unless otherwise noted, all Scripture quotations are from the New King James Version of the Bible. Copyright © 1979, 1980, 1982 by Thomas Nelson, Inc., publishers. Used by permission.

Scripture quotations marked kjv are from the King James Version of the Bible.

Scripture quotations marked niv are from the Holy Bible, New International Version. Copyright © 1973, 1978, 1984, International Bible Society. Used by permission.

Cover design by Justin Evans
Design Director: Bill Johnson

Visit the author's website at www.cfan.org.

Library of Congress Cataloging-in-Publication Data:
Bonnke, Reinhard.
  Taking action / Reinhard Bonnke.
    p. cm.
  Includes bibliographical references (p.   ).
  ISBN 978-1-61638-736-5 (trade paper) -- ISBN 978-1-61638-737-2 (e-book) 1. Gifts, Spiritual. I. Title.
  BT767.3.B66 2012
  234'.13--dc23
                              2012000779

While the author has made every effort to provide accurate telephone numbers and Internet addresses at the time of publication, neither the publisher nor the author assumes any responsibility for errors or for changes that occur after publication.

Portions of this book were originally published as *Mighty Manifestations* by Creation House, copyright © 1994, ISBN-10 0-88419-386-1; ISBN-13 978-0-88419-386-9, and *Mighty Manifestations* by Full Flame GmbH, copyright © 2002, ISBN 3-935057-00-8.

This publication is translated in Spanish under the title *Momento de actuar*, copyright © 2012 by Reinhard Bonnke, published by Casa Creación a Charisma Media company. All rights reserved.

14 15 16 17 18 — 10 9 8 7 6
Printed in the United States of America

I dedicate this book to my dear colleague and friend, the late REV. GEORGE CANTY. We were thirty years side by side, he the brilliant scholar and I the preaching evangelist. George was a fountain of blessing and inspiration to me. Fellowshiping with him was always a great encouragement. He was as my mentor, and I deeply honor his memorial.

CONTENTS

INTRODUCTION

MULTITUDES HAVE BEEN baptized in the Holy Spirit this century, as in our own ongoing gospel crusades. We regularly witness many mighty manifestations of the power and love of God. It does seem important to me to explain properly our own understanding of these events in which we have been so deeply involved.

Scripture has been our final authority. Certainly experience has helped our grasp of the things of the Spirit, but as Peter wrote, God "has given to us all things that pertain to life and godliness" (2 Pet. 1:3).

To me, and to others also, it became obvious that we must record the understanding we have of the things of the Spirit and show our conclusions arrived at through the Word, illuminated by what we have seen. One reason is that there are many books today presenting many alternative views. Variations are sure to exist unless a standard authority is accepted and agreed by which to judge all such teachings. Experience itself varies, but the Scriptures do not. There is a natural public appetite to hear the things that God has done, and a strong tendency has been exhibited to draw teaching primarily from that source, with the Word regarded only as a secondary backup, if at all.

What has been called "anecdote theology" is not new. There are theories of revival itself, for example, that have been openly claimed as based purely on studies of what has happened in the past. I was anxious about this approach as I viewed the tremendous burst of divine revival phenomena today. I decided that for us, our grounds must be the Word, and that is where we stand. This meant that our entire pneumatology (the things of the Spirit) had to be subjected to the judgment of "what the Word says" over the months as this book was put together. This was wholesome discipline. We have made the study as thorough as possible, within the compass of our means, and have also striven for clarity.

The challenge to experience must come from Scripture. Experience must not challenge Scripture or adapt Scripture to what "happens to happen." Nevertheless, readers will see that I do exemplify our teaching with things God has been doing in our evangelistic crusades.

Of course, among Christians who pray and support the nation-shaking crusades of Christ for all Nations (CfaN) there is obviously a considerable variety of viewpoints on many doctrines, including that of the Holy Spirit. I offer this exposition of the Word here as a contribution to the understanding of the work of the Holy Spirit.

When it comes to the great and prior interest of evangelism, I work with people of many different spiritual affirmations.

CfaN is an evangelist-servant to the churches wherever they labor and whatever their witness or emphasis. By their help, and their help always, and in the power of the Spirit we have been privileged to bring entire nations face-to-face personally with the gospel of Christ crucified and have thoroughly checked the outcome by the Word.

This book is our practical "thank you" for the wonderful support and encouragement of countless thousands, and it is meant to throw light on the beliefs that stimulate our operations in the harvest field. Of course it makes no pretense of being an academic treatise, but the work of countless scholars has influenced it. Nor is it a rehash of popular current teaching.

I have not written merely to sell a book or repeat unexamined what has been said before. Others will certainly have seen and said things contained in this book, but nevertheless, everything here has come from a fresh examination of the Word. It is freshly minted coinage, representing an original and independent perusal of Scripture, avoiding speculation. That has been our principle. Our purpose has been to render guidance in the present world outpouring of the Spirit and the acres of print that it daily inspires.

In fact, two lifetimes of accumulated knowledge and worldwide experience and practice lie compacted here for the benefit of readers: that of my own years of mass evangelism and also of the pioneer evangelist-writer George Canty. He has been actively involved with the whole sweep of what the Holy Spirit has been doing in this work of charismatic revival. Having personal acquaintance with leaders, and even with early Pentecostal pioneers around the globe, and having written a great deal, both history and his own scriptural and theological insights, he is perhaps in a position few others can claim to contribute to such a book as this.

When we speak of the Spirit, some matters are profound. One of the main labors has been to predigest them and express them in language that insults nobody's intelligence but that also does not presume upon previous knowledge. I have striven for a simplicity, which should not be mistaken for what is kindergarten. The least or best informed should be able to appreciate these studies.

The book is divided into two parts: the first takes a careful look at what Scripture teaches about the anointing and gifts of the Holy Spirit in general; the second looks at the specific gifts listed by the apostle Paul in 1 Corinthians 12.

May the Holy Spirit add His illumination to these pages, for the glory of God.

PART 1

CHAPTER 1

THREE PILLARS
OF WISDOM

GOD USES MANPOWER. Man needs God's power. God works when people work. These propositions are the three pillars of wisdom for this book.

Power! That is the essence of the gospel. A powerless gospel preacher is like an unwashed soap salesman. Singing, "There is power, power, wonder-working power in the precious blood of the Lamb,"[1] and then having to fast and pray for a month to get power does not add up.

At the beginning of my Christian life I had an experience of the coming of the Holy Spirit into my life, which I believe was as great as that of any disciple on the Day of Pentecost. It seemed to me that the God who fills heaven and earth crowded into my soul. I notice that Peter managed to stand up and preach, but to be honest, the physical effects of my baptism in the Spirit would certainly have been too much for me to stand and preach immediately, tremendous as my empowering was for later service.

Many write about their marvelous experiences. Purely as a matter of interest I will tell you how it happened to me, but I ought to say that nobody should think God ever gives the Spirit in exactly the same way to one as to another. It happened like this.

I was a boy of eleven in Germany when my father told me about special prayer meetings for the baptism in the Holy Spirit. Ever eager for the things of God, I begged him to take me along. Just one year earlier the Lord had called me "to one day preach the gospel in Africa"—and I knew I needed the power of the Holy Spirit to do it.

A missionary from Finland was visiting the church, and he carefully explained the truth of the baptism in the Holy Spirit. We had hardly knelt down when the power of God began to pour into and over me. Joy unspeakable filled my heart, and I began to speak in other languages as the Spirit gave me utterance. It was like a heavenly fountain opening up within me, and it is flowing even today.

Soon after this I was in a service that my father was leading with a watchful eye on his son, Reinhard. There was nothing very wrong I could do or wanted to do. I had really found Jesus and wanted to be a preacher-missionary.

Then I began to get an impulse to do something my father would not like. For no reason at all I could not stop thinking about a woman in the church who sat on the opposite side. I tried to be good, but I had this feeling stronger and stronger. It was not just in my head. It seemed to be all over me, and I tingled with it more and more, too much, like voltage steadily increasing. I tried to push it out of my mind, but the tingling current became worse.

I would have to do it, but what would she say, and what would father do? So I crouched down behind the seats and step-by-step went across to her. Then I said, "I want to pray for you."

She looked at me and said, "All right—pray for me!" I put my hand upon this grown-up woman, and something happened. The current in my body seemed to jolt right out of me and into her.

At that point my father could not help but notice, and he asked, "Reinhard, what are you doing?"

The lady answered for me. "Reinhard put his hand on me, and I felt the power of the Lord go through me, and look! I am well! I am healed!"

At that time I did not know the spiritual principles behind this healing. I did not know then that if we are obedient, there is enough power from God. That lesson, and many like it, I still had to learn. Many books tell us about the authors' lives and their special awe-inspiring visitations and revelations. This is exciting, but often it leaves people feeling that they are useless, because they have had nothing like it, and that they must be inferior to these God-used people. In this book I want you to know the real truth about the Holy Spirit.

It will amount to a great revelation in your heart and will show you what you can be in God. It is for all Christian workers, not just for those who happen to have had some rare and fantastic moment. Many people, I am certain, will be like new when they have finished reading these chapters.

To unfold the three principles named above, I shall have to begin with A-B-C. Millions of sermons are preached and heard by hundreds of millions of people. But is the effect so great? Preachers say, "The people do not do what I say." That is it, of course. Of all those who listen, how many feel like exerting themselves by putting themselves out to serve the Lord? Are the rest content to sing, worship, and enjoy a good sermon? Take this book, for example. I hope that many will enjoy and profit from it. But it is those who are "doers and not hearers only" who will really share the good things that I want to share. (See James 1:22.) I am not passing on mere knowledge, but I am trying to lead everybody into the dynamic power and blessing of God.

So, the first thing is for me to encourage you. You can be absolutely sure that God has something for you to do now and a special privileged place to put you in. You are perhaps already there but do not realize it. Many think that God has some great thing for them to do—one day. Perhaps He has, but what you are doing now is important, if you are obeying Him. There is a job to suit us, a job for which we are tailored. If you think you are not really in on these things, it is not true. Do not deprive yourself of your right and proper place in the glorious scheme of God set out in this book.

Once you realize that first point, you can move on. If God wants you to do something, He will give you the ability to do it. Very likely it may stretch you beyond what you have done before. He wants you to grow. In Christ we are bigger. Whatever lies before you, God put it there. You can move mountains. Say this to yourself—"God means me to be more than I thought I was." Do not measure what you should do by your gift; measure the gift by what you should do. It will match. God is a God specializing in the impossible and thinks only in terms of the impossible. He wants this fact to show in the lives of those who belong to Him. He commands the impossible and then makes it possible, to His glory. This book will unfold, page by page, the ways to His power.

Perhaps you wonder why God should want us to do anything at all when He has all power. It is because He loves us and likes to share His pleasures and joys with us. That is His grand design, planned that way. You may feel you are a very small instrument, but each one is vital in the full orchestrated effort. The Lord of all the earth has big things in mind, but they call for millions of helpers with varied gifts and capabilities. We are vessels so that "the power may be of God and not of us," as Paul said in 2 Corinthians 4:7. Starting from the small incident I described above, I have learned that "I can do all things through Christ who strengthens me" (Phil. 4:13).

To fulfill God's purpose we should think of ourselves as humble channels for His Word and Spirit. A copper pipe cannot boast of the water that flows to the tap in our homes. We are to let the living waters flow—just stay unblocked. Whatever gifts or talents we lay at His feet, the Master can use. They become accessory parts, shaping the channel through which God does what He wants. That is a lesson we must learn well and take deep into our heart as the basis of everything else we learn or do.

God has given me my job. Many a time I have been asked, "When did you begin to see miracles in your ministry, and why do so many turn to Christ when you preach?" The answer is found in what I have just said—God gives us the power to do what He commands. That comes through the baptism with the Holy Spirit.

I experienced that wonderful baptism, and it stayed with me, thrusting and surging within me. I spoke with tongues also, and it was such a marvelous thing to me that I have never doubted since that miracles are for today. Of course, I had had faith before. The Word itself has always stirred my faith. Then, when the promise of the Spirit was fulfilled for me and it became an ongoing constant filling, the whole experience boosted my faith like supercharging a car engine. The Bible confirmed what was happening.

WHEN THE SPIRIT COMES

Next I want you to ponder a well-known promise. Let me write out what it really says. You may be too familiar with it but have lost sight of its tremendous wonder, for it is one of the most impossible and fantastic expectations any person ever entertained.

> You shall be baptized with the Holy Spirit not many days from now....You shall receive power when the Holy Spirit has come upon you.
> —ACTS 1:5, 8

Could it really happen in our time? Well, it did for me. I cannot think of anything more wonderful for human beings than that. It means being filled with God. It is not getting high on God, a sort of euphoric, giddy happiness, all froth and bubble. The Holy Spirit is not a super-drug, a tranquilizer, or a stimulant. He does not come to give us an emotional experience, but make no mistake about it, His presence is heart moving. Life is tough. God sends His power to people in tough situations. He is the original life force meant for us all.

Over the years I have come to understand more and more. Fresh revelation has burst upon me. It is all so wonderful. God wants me to share it with the whole world in my preaching, and now especially in this book.

CHRISTIANITY: WHAT IS IT?

Did you know that when people talk of Christianity as a world religion they are quite wrong? A religion is a system, and Jesus left no system. It is more than just a faith to be believed. The real thing is actually divine power in action. Christian truth cannot simply be written down like so many facts or definitions. Christian truth is alive. You cannot write a person down and say, "That's her!" You cannot write Christianity down and say, "That's it!" It is a living entity. The breath of God animates the gospel, or it is a dead body of truth instead of living truth. Jesus said, "I am the way, the truth, and the life" (John 14:6). That is how I know it, and that is how I preach it. Who would not want to preach a gospel like that?

Now let us try to make an up-to-date definition of Christianity, as charismatic Pentecostals understand it. It is the Holy Spirit in action making the Word of God happen. We must be able to show people that the gospel is what it claims to be. When a world-class athlete stands on the track, we do not need to argue to prove that he is a champion. Just fire the starting pistol! That is what I do—the gospel of Christ is alive, so I go into a stadium and let the gospel do its own thing, and everybody can see it is alive. That is what the Holy Spirit does.

POWERS OF A NEW ORDER

I have seen countless mighty wonders wrought and unclean spirits cast out by the finger of God. Christ explained it. "If I cast out demons with the finger of God, surely the kingdom of God has come upon you" (Luke 11:20).

We must look carefully at that explanation. The kingdom, what is it? If we are to catch the real secret of the faith, we must understand the kingdom. Jesus talked about it all the time. We only need to consider it from one angle at present.

Now, we have had different historical ages—the Stone Age, the Dark Ages, and so on. These periods were given a special name to show their main features. Then we have the Christian age, with each year being designated A.D.—*Anno Domini*, which means "in the year of our Lord." Is it just another division of history? No. This age is unique. The Christian age is when another age also broke in—the kingdom of God. Jesus began to preach, "Repent, for the kingdom of God is at hand" (Matt. 4:17).

The kingdom is the realm of God, in which God's power is supreme. When Christ came, He introduced the activity of God the Holy Spirit into our mundane affairs. It is a new resource, not physical power like water, wind, or nuclear energy, which are all part of the natural scene. This was the power of a world with laws far above the laws of nature.

Read the following statements carefully: In the beginning God made this world by the powers of another world.

In Christ Jesus He reintroduced the powers of that creative world into the earthly scene. That is the kingdom of God.

I will explain more in chapter 2, but we should grasp now that our world has been invaded, and the authority of the kingdom of God has drawn near to us. It is a superior order, a miracle order, overarching the natural or scientific order. Higher laws can overrule the physical laws. The spiritual can overrule the material. That happens in the baptism of the Holy Spirit and when His gifts operate.

John 1:1–3 says that all things were made by the Word; that is, by the Son of God. John 1:14 states, "The Word became flesh." He who was the source of everything we see came into His own creation. He is the one who "came down from heaven" (John 6:38, KJV). That statement "came down from heaven" is very important. It means that He became the bridge reaching from the invisible world to the visible. In John 1:51, Jesus portrays Himself as a Jacob's ladder set up between earth and heaven.

There are two orders, with their own forces or powers. Jesus is the link between them, the heavenly and the earthly order. The power of heaven is the creative power of God by which the earth was made. So through Christ—the link with heaven—things are possible on earth that were not possible before He came. He is called "the new and living way." There are two dimensions: the dimension beneath the sun and the dimension above the sun. Through Jesus Christ and by the

Holy Spirit, commerce has begun between earth and heaven. The angels of God are coming and going.

Through the breaking in of Christ into our world, God can exercise His will here, through our prayers. It is a case, as we said, of God wanting manpower and us needing God's power, for Jesus taught us to pray, "Your will be done on earth as it is in heaven" (Matt. 6:10). He has not shut Himself out of any part of His universe. He is Lord. He applies greater forces, and the natural laws obey by the Spirit of God. We call that a miracle. This age is a new "dispensation"; God deals with us in a new way. There is, of course, a grand purpose behind it. The object is not to pull off a few sensational wonders, like stage tricks, but the redemption of the world.

If you have ever thought about it, every time you move, you bring natural laws under your control. Left to nature, rocks would not fly. Human beings introduce a higher law, that of their will, and they can throw rocks and make them fly. We are not the slaves of the laws of nature; they are our slaves. We can make them obey us. We can use the scientific laws to leave this planet altogether. We can move into a state of weightlessness or even fly to the moon.

When people say that miracles are contrary to the laws of nature, it completely ignores the fact that, where there is a superior will and superior power—even that of man as well as omnipotent God—all the laws of nature can be overridden. The only difficulty is when people do not believe in God. Bring God into it, and nothing is impossible. That is what has happened. The kingdom of God is among us; therefore devils are cast out, the sick are healed, and we speak with tongues.

There is another fact to be faced. What really are human beings? We are both flesh and spirit. God linked us to two worlds: the earthly and the spiritual. By our five senses we are aware of this physical world, and by our spirit we sense the nonphysical world—and on occasions fear it, as a haunted house.

But things have gone wrong. The great calamity has befallen us. Sin has almost destroyed the link between body and spirit. After the fall of Adam only occasional flashes of the supernatural were seen until Jesus came. Only a breakthrough now and then is recorded in the Old Testament. Sometimes God exercised His sovereignty and initiated a spate of wonders, as with Moses and the ministry of Elijah and Elisha. God's power and His authority were rarely seen directly.

Then a radical change was effected. Christ's marvelous coming, God in the flesh, opened up the resources of creative power. He was, and is, Lord of all things. He announced it Himself, saying, "The kingdom of God is at hand" (Mark 1:15).

At this point we come to the phrase "born again." One of the possibilities that Christ opened up was to be born again. This Greek expression can also be translated "born from above." Men and women can be made new—new creatures, the Bible says—by the powers of heaven, the kingdom power of God.

Obviously a person born from above would never be satisfied with a world that was gross and only material. They need spiritual links as well as physical ones. The present world, with its limited scientific laws, is not big enough for a converted Christian, anymore than a cage is for an eagle. It needs extending, and that extension is into the fourth dimension beyond our three-dimensional world. We "walk in the Spirit" (Gal. 5:25). God has "made us sit together in the heavenly places in Christ Jesus" (Eph. 2:6).

The Book of Acts shows men beginning to draw upon new resources and to move through the world blessing the people with salvation and healing. The first new men in Christ, new creatures of the kingdom, were sent out to bring others into the same kingdom order, with new instincts, new powers, and new laws written on their heart. (See Hebrews 8.)

After I was baptized in the Spirit and spoke with tongues, it did not take me long to realize that this gift opened up new possibilities. If, through the Spirit, I spoke with tongues, then through the Spirit there could be other wonders. I have learned to live in the Spirit. I am on new ground where signs and wonders happen. Praise God!

If it was not for that, nothing could happen as it does. Vast multitudes come to my meetings. They represent a daunting accumulation of needs. But I am baptized in the Holy Spirit. I know the powers of the coming age and how to tap into those resources. A great conviction grips me that God has something for them. That is not my private secret, but it's also that of hundreds of millions today. If I have any other secret, it is the message itself. I am confident in its effectiveness. It is "the power of God to salvation" (Rom. 1:16).

A GOSPEL THAT ISN'T

If what we have been teaching so far is not what some readers had thought, we have to say that the gospel is being reinterpreted today in ways that take the heart out of it—and out of us. Liberal and rationalistic thought is based on the shifting sand of biblical criticism, speculation, and philosophy. No assured grounds for the frightened millions have ever been offered by this new thought. It is a theology of chaff, a diet of starvation for the God-hungry. Too many scholars have made truth depend on questions that can never have any certain answer, never reach finality—guesswork that is foredoomed to do absolutely nothing for lost nations and devil-stricken masses. If God is the only Savior, He cannot save by a message of "perhaps," or "if," or "it is my opinion." The world needs people with a live link to heaven.

For all classes, no matter how cultured, or how primitive, there is one Word of truth—the Cross—to the wise, to the barbarian, to Greek and Jew, to everyone. The gospel is the power of God. The gospel preacher is an ambassador demanding surrender to the kingdom of heaven. It is God's ultimatum. He shows us the way things are. The gospel is neither a theory nor an abstraction, but it is the reality behind everything. We either recognize it or perish.

When you grasp what we are saying here, then you join the army with the battering ram of the Word of the Cross. It will pulverize the strongholds of the devil. It is the drumroll thunder of God's invincible army on the march. When God filled me with His Spirit and opened my lips to speak with tongues, He opened my ears to hear the triumphant peal of the trumpet announcing that Jesus has all power in heaven and on earth. What a gift!

A GOD IDENTIFIED BY MIRACLES

At this point I think I should illustrate what we have declared by actual examples. Once, during a service in Brazzaville, the capital of the Republic of Congo, God gave me a word of knowledge for a couple, otherwise unknown to me, somewhere among the tens of thousands present. There was a woman who had been in a coma for three days and had been carried into the meeting by her husband. By faith and in obedience to God's prompting, I told the vast audience what the Spirit of the Lord had made known to me. As I spoke, the unconscious woman, though not hearing, came out of her coma and was healed. Mind over matter? Impossible— the patient knew nothing of what was going on until she revived.

Another poor soul also present needed urgent surgery. Her unborn baby had died in her womb, and the hospital had arranged for it to be removed the next day. When a prayer was offered for the mass of needy ones in the service, the baby in her womb leaped. She rushed forward to the platform tearfully to testify, and only just in time, because straight afterward she went into labor and was taken away to give birth to a bouncing baby boy.

These are not the only wonders that have left me almost unable to sleep for excitement and joy. Infinitely greater is that the Holy Spirit sweeps through the vast crowds assembled to hear the Word of God like a mighty heavenly damburst and lifts them on a wave of blessing into the kingdom of God.

THE CROSS AND KINGDOM MIRACLES

The last of the basic things in this chapter is this: I have to show you that the power of the kingdom, the Holy Spirit, and the gospel of the Cross are so welded together that they cannot be separated. It was the work of Christ, especially in His death, that tore down the wall between this world and the other world of the kingdom of God. Since then the Holy Spirit has invested everything in the crucified Christ. He works His wonders only on redemption ground. The Spirit supports only the gospel, always and everywhere.

What more do we need? One man filled with the Spirit is better than a hundred committees that "keep minutes but lose hours." When God so loved the world, He did not form a committee but sent His Son, and His Son sent the Spirit.

Christ said that believers are the light of the world, but the Holy Spirit is needed to switch them on.

No doubt many reading this book are keen for miracles. There is nothing wrong with that. I want to help, and it will save many from disillusionment if I inform them that miracles belong only to the gospel—nothing else. There are no marvels for the sake of marvels; God is not a showman. He is not in the business of supplying marvels to bring acclaim to any strutting egotist. The Holy Spirit is in league with the crucified Christ—even linked in name, the Spirit of Christ. They have one mind—to defeat the devil through the gospel.

The Spirit finds fulfillment only in the gospel. The gospel is so big. It is totally comprehensive, leaving nothing untouched—visible or invisible; earth, hell, or heaven. Theologian George Lindbeck in his book *The Nature of Doctrine* says, "A scriptural world is thus able to absorb the universe."[2]

As a Christian, I knew that the Cross had a spiritual effect in my life, but when I spoke with tongues, it reached me as an earthly person. The Father in heaven and the Son on earth were concerned with redemption, each in their sphere, as Jesus expressed in His prayer:

> I have glorified You on earth. I have finished the work which You have given Me to do. And now, O Father, glorify Me together with Yourself, with the glory which I had with You before the world was.
>
> —JOHN 17:4–5

These verses tell us that Christ's work on earth affected earth and that the Father's work affected glory. Jesus came here, for here. Hallelujah! If it was to get us an entrance into heaven only, He might have arranged it in heaven; but salvation had to be produced on earth for earthly purposes. My baptism in the Spirit touched both my spirit and my body, typical of the true nature of the Christian faith.

This truth makes all true Christian doctrine shine brighter. Salvation is not for part of a man but for the whole man. It is seen for example in healing, which is a spiritual and physical operation.

The Old Testament stresses the link between sickness and sin, and also the link between healing and forgiveness. That is a truth refined in the New Testament. We shall come to that when considering the gifts of healings.

CHAPTER 2

GOD HAS
TAKEN THE FIELD

OUR FIRST CHAPTER showed us that the Christian age is also a new-power age. A famous historian's words are interesting. Arthur Toynbee in his *Study of History* talks about "a new creative power flowing back into the historical process."[1] This is the kind of creative power that Jesus brought into the world. It is the Holy Spirit. The present expansion of churches, which allow the Holy Spirit free expression, is the greatest religious phenomenon of our age, as *Time* magazine reported in 1971—and that was only at the beginning of the greatest thrust.

Living in this world is different since Jesus came. There is a new resource. The world of physical law has been impacted by the spiritual laws of the world to come. The results are with us. The Gospels introduce it, and the Acts of the

Apostles first reports men and women accepting it. We shall now look at some other aspects of this great change.

THE HOLY SPIRIT KINGDOM POWER

The Father gave us two gifts, both personal and equal—first His Son and then His Spirit. Jesus ranked the Spirit alongside Himself, describing Him as "another Comforter" (John 14:16, KJV). Christ said it was better for the Spirit to come than for He Himself to be with us in the flesh. The Holy Spirit's commission is to take the place of Christ. Jesus healed the sick, for example, and the Holy Spirit follows the pattern of Christ.

How do we know who the Spirit is? The Holy Spirit is God in action. Whenever there are supernatural operations, they are by the Spirit. All divine manifestations, such as the gifts, are always by the Spirit. When God moved on the world in the beginning, it was by His Spirit. "The Spirit of God was hovering over the face of the waters" (Gen. 1:2). The Father's will is spoken by the Word and performed by the Spirit. He is the "executive" of the Godhead.

The only Spirit that Jesus promised us is the miracle Spirit, the Holy Spirit. There is no non-miracle Holy Spirit. To claim to possess the Holy Spirit and deny the very work that has always distinguished Him can only grieve Him. He is who began with the supreme physical wonder of creating the world. He does not change His nature. What He was, He is and always will be—God operating on the earthly scene. "I

AM WHO I AM" (Exod. 3:14). The Holy Spirit, who made the world supernaturally, should have no difficulty in continuing supernaturally.

John the Baptist, the divinely sent forerunner introducing Christ, proclaimed a new era. "Repent, for the kingdom of heaven is at hand" (Matt. 3:2). The central core of that proclamation was the Messiah baptizing in the Holy Spirit. It was far greater than the restoration of Israeli greatness—it was nothing less than a cosmic change. John unfolded a map of the future showing a river not of water but of fire. In Matthew 3:11 John used an earthly element, water, but Christ baptizes in a heavenly element, divine fire.

Jesus picks up and echoes the same words: "John truly baptized with water, but you shall be baptized with the Holy Spirit not many days from now" (Acts 1:5). We should take note of the fact that Jesus did not baptize anybody with the Spirit while He was on earth. John preached to people from "all the land of Judea, and those from Jerusalem . . . and [they] were all baptized by him in the Jordan River, confessing their sins" (Mark 1:5). It was to this indiscriminate mass of people that John preached and declared "I indeed baptized you with water, but He will baptize you with the Holy Spirit" (v. 8). John laid down no special qualifications except repentance.

MANY BAPTISMS

Before continuing, we must look at another theory. The theory has been propounded that the whole church was baptized in the Spirit forever on the Day of Pentecost. Individuals can seek to be filled for themselves, however, but one filling of the Spirit is not lasting or enough, and we need to keep coming for a repeat experience—"many fillings."

But if the whole church was baptized forever on the Day of Pentecost, why are Christians supposed to seek many fillings? We might ask if anyone listening to John or Christ ever dreamed they meant such a thing. We cannot direct you to a scripture that argues such a thing, because there is not a single word about "repeated fillings." Neither is there the slightest suggestion that there would be a distinct baptism exclusively for an elite band of the early disciples by proxy for the church of all time. Whether the Spirit comes at new birth or not, the first believers enjoyed a personal experience of the indwelling Spirit, and nothing less than that is offered to all who believe from the Day of Pentecost onward.

John plainly announced the purpose of Christ—to baptize men and women in the Spirit. It would characterize Him, giving Him the name of Baptizer, just as John was the Baptist. Nobody could pretend that a single performance shows what we are. I once baked a cake, but it is not typical of me, and I would need a lot of urging to attempt it again. They do not call me a baker because of my sole Madeira success. I would have to bake cakes daily to bear the name of baker. Christ is called the Baptizer because that is His constant work, His heavenly office, the Baptizer in the Holy Spirit, "the same yesterday, today, and forever" (Heb. 13:8).

For those readers who would perhaps want a more technical explanation, here is what Ronald W. Foulkes, commissioned by the Methodist Charismatic Fellowship of Tasmania, says in *The Flame Shall Not Be Quenched*. We quote it here, including his comments on Greek grammar.

> There is a cliché, "One baptism, many fillings," but we should realize this is not scriptural; the biblical pattern and provision is for constant fullness, one is to go on being filled. The word *filled* is in a verbal form known as "ingressive aorist," suggesting an entrance into a state of condition. It is clear that the Christian who is baptized does not enter into a transitory experience, but into an abiding condition of fullness. Luke elaborates on the effect when speaking of Peter; he describes him as one "filled with the Holy Spirit" (Acts 4:8), using the passive participle of the aorist tense, indicating a happening in process.[2]

You will no doubt hear people talk about "one baptism, many fillings." Remember it is the code word of those who oppose the baptism in the Spirit with signs following. If, however, charismatics or Pentecostals talk like this, let us ask a simple question: When someone says that they have been baptized in the Spirit, how long does it last? A week? An hour? Six months? Does the Holy Spirit leak away like power from a car battery? Is the baptism with the Spirit only one drink, and we need to go for another and another, like cups of tea? Another question: How should we know when the Spirit has gone and we need another renewal? For how long can we say, "I am Spirit-filled"? What signs are there when we are and when we are not?

Jesus said that when the Comforter has come, He will "abide with you forever" (John 14:16). This is where the blessing of speaking with tongues is seen. We cannot speak unless the Holy Spirit gives us utterance, and if He does, He is there. By that sign we can go out and conquer, for He is with us. The Spirit abides with us. Our feelings are always an unreliable power meter.

History helps us here. In the nineteenth century, before tongues were commonly heard, the problem was to know when the Spirit had come. People relied on intense and highly sensational moments. They would pray a great deal, believing that power could be measured by the time spent in prayer, an idea quite foreign to the Bible. At the dawn of the twentieth century, for the first time it was taught that the sign of tongues (glossolalia) was the assurance of the coming of the Spirit. This immediately triggered off the sweeping power of the greatest movement of the Holy Spirit of all time. My own faith was activated by the initial sign of tongues, which led me into this present ministry of evangelism.

We shall learn more from Jesus. He spoke to the woman at the well in Samaria and referred to "whoever drinks" (John 4:14). The Greek tense He used (aorist) means to drink once only, not keep coming back with an empty water pot. That was the very thing the woman at the well of Sychar understood, and she said, "I need not come to the well to draw."

The one drink results in a fountain of water springing up into everlasting life. Water is always the symbol of the Holy Spirit.

ANOTHER COMFORTER

One thing has always amazed me. The disciples did not weep when Christ left them. They never showed any nostalgic longings, and they never talked of the good old days. Luke tells us that after Jesus ascended out of sight, they "returned to Jerusalem with great joy, and were continually in the temple praising and blessing God" (Luke 24:52–53). Why did they display such a remarkable reaction to the departure of Jesus? The answer is—the coming of the Spirit. When Christ was present, they were only eyewitnesses of His power. But when the Day of Pentecost came, they were more than eyewitnesses. They possessed power themselves and experienced the divine presence personally, which was different from Christ being with them.

Now that personal sense of the presence of God is nowhere said to be just for them, the disciples alone, an elite band. Peter said otherwise: "The promise is to you and to your children, and to all who are afar off, as many as the Lord our God will call" (Acts 2:39). He quoted the promise from Joel 2:28, where God says "I will pour out My Spirit." Wesley's *Explanatory Notes Upon the New Testament* says of this verse: "Not on the Day of Pentecost only, upon all flesh—on persons of every age, sex, and rank."[3] It describes the normal Christian experience, as does the whole Book of Acts.

Another curious fact is that although Jesus told the disciples to take bread and wine in memory of Him, they never used the "language of remembering." One does not remember a person one lives with. Jesus was a living and abiding presence by the Spirit. "Therefore, from now on, we regard no one according to the flesh. Even though we have known Christ according to the flesh, yet now we know Him thus no longer" (2 Cor. 5:16). To be filled with the Spirit brings us alive to Jesus, which is far better than being alive when Jesus was on earth.

Note too that the Spirit does not come to talk about Himself but to reveal Jesus (John 16:15). Paul said he preached Christ crucified in the power and demonstration of the Spirit. If we only preach the power of the Spirit without the Cross, it is a short circuit, which brings a loss of the very power we preach. The Spirit's primary interest is in the Cross. We do not preach power but the gospel, which is the power of God by the Spirit.

SPIRIT GALVANIZED

Speaking at a conference, Donald Gee said that the Spirit was not "the subject of theological dogma but a burning experience." He pointed out that when Paul dealt with problems in Galatia, his appeal was to their experience (Gal. 3:2). The Holy Spirit was God in earthly activity as Jesus had been.

The baptism in the Spirit was not meant to be a single, emotional event recorded in believers' diaries. It wraps around believers permanently. The Spirit is their environment, the air that they breathe moment by moment, providing the vitality of the Christian faith. When we bombard the world with the gospel, the Holy Spirit is the explosive ammunition for our artillery. The Spirit animates believers, their teachings, their preaching, their prayer, their service, and their very lives.

The Holy Spirit is the dynamic of the faith. Without the life of the Holy Spirit, Christianity is just another lifeless religious system that can only be kept going by human effort. But nothing can compete with the Holy Spirit. We cannot do without the Holy Spirit no matter what we substitute, whether organization, church magnificence, prestige, education, or any other factor on which reliance has been placed.

WHEN WE KNOW—DO!

We have now gone a little way in our studies. Let me pause a moment to remind you that God Himself teaches us when we obey Him. If we learn these things, then we must understand that the Holy Spirit, God in action, leads us into action. We were not saved just to linger in fond contentment, happy that we are saved, holding meetings to congratulate one another on our good fortune that we are redeemed.

There are higher activities than church celebrations, Christian pop concerts, and endless new worship songs—Christian as they may be. Our Lord is worthy to be praised indeed, but worship choruses alone will never save the world, especially those songs that make no mention of the name of Jesus nor have any gospel content. Praise is not the power of God unto salvation. The gospel is the power of God. We must not flatter ourselves that we can build a throne for God with lots of new songbooks. Our commission from God contains the clause "Preach the Word." "It pleased God through the foolishness of the message preached to save those who believe" (1 Cor. 1:21).

We should do more than celebrate. We must communicate. Richard John Neuhaus says, "We are not celebrating our securities and satisfactions. We are celebrating the perilous business of love—of that supreme love that did not and does not turn back from the Cross."[4]

Some have said that there is more about fellowship than evangelism in the New Testament. This is a superficial count of words. In any case there is no *fellowship* without evangelism. The word fellowship (Greek: *koinonia*) is much more than meeting our Christian friends in cozy comfort for the "ample interchange of sweet discourse." It is sharing. We share the gospel and the fullness of the Spirit so that others have what we can have. *Koinonia* depends on evangelism.

RIVERS

Returning again to what Scripture says about the Holy Spirit, the word *rivers* is used repeatedly. It describes the ideal for

believers and is symbolic of the Holy Spirit. It was antici-
pated in Isaiah 58:11: "You shall be...like a spring of water,
whose waters do not fail." A "rivers" experience requires the
miracle presence of the Holy Spirit. For many people in our
temperate Western climate, exuberance is foreign, unnatural,
and embarrassing. For those, however, who stand within the
kingdom of God, the culture of the world matters little. In
our kingdom people shout for joy.

The Septuagint (the Greek version of the Old Testament)
uses a surprising word about the Spirit of God acting in the
lives of Samson and Saul. It says the Spirit "leapt" upon
them. This rare word (*allomai*) is used twice in Acts 3:8 in
the healing of the lame man—"leaping up" (Greek: *exal-
lomai*) and "leaping" (Greek: *hallomai*). Leaping life and
dancing waters are the biblical scenario.

The Hebrew word for "worship" signifies bodily action.
Those blessed by the mighty Spirit of God, who "leap for joy,"
are bound to appear strange. It is not surprising when people
who have not been in the Upper Room of Pentecost, but
only in the church supper room, deride Spirit-filled people
as "enthusiasts and fanatics." The onlookers in Jerusalem
thought that the apostles were drunk, being completely ignorant of the facts of the case.

Those apostles had critics. We should never be worried
by critics. There has never yet been a doctrine or teaching,
or anybody doing anything, but that somebody thought
they knew better. The writer R. Knox, for example, showed

contempt for John Wesley as a mere "enthusiast"—meaning an overwrought or unbalanced person. Father Knox may be an example of cool scholarship, but from his book *Enthusiasm*, he will strike nobody as a man who had been with the 120 on the Day of Pentecost, or stood shoeless at the burning bush with Moses, or with Joshua before the Man with the drawn sword. The intellectual Bishop of Bristol told Wesley that he considered "the pretending to extraordinary revelations and gifts of the Holy Ghost is a horrid thing, a very horrid thing."[5]

Ronald Foulkes refers to a writer saying in 1849: "We admit that Wesley was an enthusiast, but only to the degree in which a man more than ordinarily filled with the Holy Ghost would be an enthusiast."[6] Wesley's first rule for stewards of the Methodist Society, quoting Ephesians 3:16, was "You are to be men full of the Holy Ghost."[7] At a meeting with George Whitefield in Fetter Lane on January 1, 1739, at three o'clock in the morning: "At the hour mentioned, the power of God came upon them so mightily, that many cried out for exceeding joy, others fell prostrate on the ground."[8]

We only need to ask one question: If Christ did exactly what He promised and baptized people in the Holy Spirit and fire, what would they be like? Cool, restrained, self-contained? With glory currents of divine radiance flowing through them, would they sit, as Shakespeare said, "like his grandsire carved in alabaster"?[9] The emblem of God is fire, not a watermelon.

Who are the most ridiculous—the people dancing for joy with the vision of God, or the people posing unperturbed like the Sphinx, which was unmoved even when Napoleon fired a cannon at it? Flesh and blood are not granite to experience the Spirit and show no sign of it. What we have in earthen vessels is "treasure" in order to show that this all-surpassing power is from God (2 Cor. 4:7). Something totally strange will be evident to minds alienated from God, like Festus said to Paul: "You are beside yourself. Much learning is driving you mad!" (Acts 26:24). How else could it be today when people experience the original brand of Christianity and not some diluted, de-gutted, tranquilized, sentimentalized version of it? "You He made alive," we read in Ephesians 2:1, not "You He stiffened."

We will look again at this matter of rivers. In John 7:37–38, Jesus cried, "If anyone thirsts, let him come to Me and drink. He who believes in Me, as the Scripture has said, out of his heart will flow rivers of living water." There are no commas in the Greek original. So we should read it like this: "He who believes in Me as the Scripture has said." That is, rivers of living water will flow from those "who believe in Me as the Scripture has said." It is not living waters that the Scripture talks about but Jesus Himself, and those who believe on him. People have not found which scripture Jesus had in mind when He spoke of waters, though we have suggested one above—Isaiah 58:11. The promise of living water originates with Jesus Himself, and as Peter preached, "The promise is to you and to your children, and to all who are afar off, as many as the Lord our God will call" (Acts 2:39).

It is even more important to look again at John 3:34. The correct translation of this verse reads, "God does not give the Spirit by measure." The giving is not limited. It is given to us all, as John 1:16 tells us: "Of His fullness we have all received." Literally "because of His fullness" we are filled without measure.

Fullness lies in Christ Jesus and flows out of Him to fill us. He is the source. In Acts 2:17 Peter quoted Joel 2:28, speaking of God pouring out of His Spirit. The word is "from" His Spirit (Greek: *apo*). So long as Christ is full, we shall "be being filled." He is "full of grace and truth" (John 1:14), and out of it we receive grace for grace, that is, grace constantly being renewed.

We are not set up in business all on our own with a lump sum of spiritual capital and power resources, which make us independent. We are not self-sufficient little Christs, replicas of the Son of God, who alone had immortality. Those who teach such a thing manifest gross theological ignorance at the very least. We receive moment by moment "out of" Christ's fullness, like the branches of a vine receive sap. We are not vines ourselves living separate existences, but we are complete in Him (Col. 2:10).

THE SPIRIT'S DIFFERENCE

The prophets struggled in vain to bring Israel back to God. But when Peter preached, full of the Spirit, three thousand people surrendered. Without the Holy Spirit, Christianity is reduced to "religion," which is no more effective than the Old Testament system and the priesthood before the age of the Spirit.

Jesus said, "You shall receive power when the Holy Spirit has come upon you" (Acts 1:8). Without that vitality we have a secularized, nominalized, rationalized, and harmless religion. Mystical contemplation bears no resemblance to New Testament dynamism; quietism is for Buddhists, not Christians.

Before the charismatics arrived, there were those who were fired up and Spirit filled or "pneumatized." Whatever chill may have frozen the church, however much "enthusiasm" was disapproved, and Christianity was only "churchianity," there were always some lively Spirit-filled people around. The springs of spiritual waters in this century came from rains centuries before. Some trace them to Wesley and his teaching, which he called "perfect love," but whatever it was called, the vision or experience Wesley had came from earlier men and women of God.

CALL IT WHAT YOU LIKE

Many different terms are used for the same experiences in Scripture. All the terms, such as "coming upon," "being filled," "drinking," and "anointing," describe the same divine gift. Christ said we should "ask, seek, knock" for the Spirit (Luke 11:9–13). Those who receive the Spirit in New Testament style surely have a right to call their experience by a New Testament name.

The "baptism in the Holy Spirit" is a New Testament expression used by both John the Baptist and Jesus. The personal experience of millions conforms to the New Testament promise, whether it is called baptism or anything else. If it looks like a baptism, sounds like it, feels like it, and operates like it, what else is it? It cannot be argued out of existence by debates about what to call it. If we do what the apostles did and we get what the apostles got, its name does not matter.

There has been opposition, and there still is. It does seem suspicious, however, that nobody invented any teaching against an after-conversion receiving of the Spirit, until after the "tongues people" began to be noticed. History shows that the church had always assumed that to receive the Holy Spirit was a separate experience. From the earliest times when people were baptized, they were anointed afterward to receive the Spirit. It was called the *chrism*.[10] The litanies of various kinds showed that chrism, the anointing with oil, was given only to those baptized and said to be children of God and in the kingdom. A candidate was considered unfit to receive the Spirit until regenerated. In the Anglican Church, confirmation after baptism has been taken as the moment when the Spirit is imparted by the laying on of hands by the bishop.

Let us look at this a little further. If everyone received the Spirit by proxy on the Day of Pentecost, as some teach, why do they pray for the many fillings? What use was the baptism on the Day of Pentecost if each person needs filling again and again? And, of course, what seems to be overlooked is that all these fillings are after-conversion experiences.

There is one thing we should not overlook. Some receive a mighty baptism at the same time as conversion, as did Cornelius and his household in Acts 10, but not everyone did or does. When one receives it, whether at new birth, as some argue, or later, that does not alter the fact that this great experience actually exists. For the disciples it came later, as it has for millions of others.

If the enduement with the Holy Spirit and power always comes with the new birth, we wonder why those who say so still seek God for power. If the baptism of the Spirit takes place at conversion for everybody, does it look like it? The secret of the great revivalists and of the sweeping power of the present spiritual outpouring has been some kind of further experience or experiences in which God came in an extraordinary way.

THE EFFECT OF THE SPIRIT

We now go on to see what the effects of being filled with the Spirit should be. To be filled with the Spirit is shown in the New Testament, and in the lives of millions, to have a dynamic and energizing effect, or "power" (Greek: *dunamis*). There is little Scripture to suggest the Spirit comes upon men like a quiet breath, unobtrusive and unnoticed. It is usually very noticeable—such as manifestations of the Spirit, fire, wind, noise, wonders, outward signs, powers, and visible effects. God does not give His gifts to the unconverted, nor does He give His Holy Spirit to the world, but when we are born again, we are encouraged to be filled, just as Paul admonished the churches (Eph. 5:18).

I must remind you again that we are looking at what Scripture says about these things. Some turn to church history. They try to prove that apostolic power died out with the apostles. Church history, not the Bible, settles their doctrine. They could profitably have wondered why it died down at the end of the apostolic age (though in fact it did not completely vanish). There is not a single scrap of biblical evidence to indicate that it should have done. A true scholar would want to know the answer. If we take anything from church history, we know that unbelief and spiritual decline set in, and the power of the Spirit was therefore unlikely to be widely manifested.

Christianity was never intended to be anything else but

an outpouring of the Spirit. It is a reviving, quickening, renewing energy. Revival is not an extraordinary work beyond normal Christianity. Christianity is revival. There are not two Spirits, the Spirit received at new birth and the Spirit of revival, which, they say, sometimes comes down from heaven and takes the field. The Spirit of God took the field long ago and has never withdrawn from the battle. He does not visit it now and then, but He comes permanently. Having put His hand to the plough, He does not look back. "Revival" is always there when the Word is preached and the Spirit is present.

Both David and Isaiah prayed, "Lord, rend the heavens and come down." (See Psalm 144:5; Isaiah 64:1.) It happened when Jesus came. New Testament believers need never pray it again. Christ tore the heavens and came down to us. He then returned through the heavens, ensuring that they remain open. The rent heavens have been rent forever and have never been sewn up again, neither by a needle-wielding Satan nor any other hand. Through that open heaven the Holy Spirit then began to descend—the latter rain. The heavens are no more like brass. Hell cannot impose sanctions and blockade the kingdom of God, nor can it deprive the citizens of heaven. The new and living way is established beyond enemy control.

In his book *Joy Unspeakable* Dr. Martyn Lloyd-Jones concluded that revival is the baptism in the Holy Spirit.[11] He lays down firm proof that there is a scriptural reception of power after conversion, that it is the baptism with the Spirit, and that it is revival. Since 1901, when that truth was recovered, the restoration of biblical signs and wonders has brought hundreds of millions into the kingdom of God.

No New Testament Christian was a contemplative. Mystics usually end up with new teachings, which are error. The apostles were activists. Smith Wigglesworth was right: "The Acts of the Apostles was written because the apostles acted."[12] They did not visit shrines or keep the relics of holy men. They were in vital contact with God themselves through the Spirit and went direct to Him, not through saints and their bones.

The entire Christian life is "in the Spirit." By the Spirit, the Son of God is the Anointed One. This set the pattern. Just as He went about doing good because He was anointed with the Spirit, so must we all. We are told to walk (as Jesus did everywhere) in the Spirit, pray in the Spirit, love in the Spirit, live in the Spirit, be filled with the Spirit, sing in the Spirit, and have the fruit of the Spirit.

The Spirit-filled life is not an experience to be cultivated in special conditions like indoor crocuses. Christians are not flowers. During the early expansion of the industrial cities of England some clergymen could not be persuaded to take a parish among the hordes of unwashed workers, because they said it might spoil their "spirituality." The Holy Spirit makes believers tough specimens for all conditions. They carry perpetual springtime in their soul and are "winterized" (as

Americans describe the preparation of their homes for the cold weather).

The apostles discovered a new resilience, a new strength within them, and a power that operated in their weakness, which sent them out into a brutalized, pagan world to demolish its idol establishment and change history. That is a true mark of "the Spirit-filled life."

Things like that are happening today. A new age of persecution is testing the church over half the earth. We may have to lay down our physical lives, but we are proving that the baptism in the Spirit makes people unconquerable.

CHAPTER 3

THE ANOINTING

H OLY SPIRIT ANOINTING is fully scriptural. In the Old Testament all who served God had to be anointed. This is replaced in the New Testament by the Holy Spirit for all believers.

The first thing to learn is that "anointing" is just one of the synonyms of the baptism in the Spirit; there are others.

For years we have sung with Psalm 23, "My head Thou dost with oil anoint," which actually refers to the practice of oiling the head of sheep for their protection; but the anointing of the Spirit, or the baptism with the Spirit, is more than merely a protective health measure.[1]

Let us see what we can learn in the house of Simon the Pharisee (Luke 7:36–50). Jesus is making a complaint using language similar to that of Psalm 23. He is saying to His host, "You did not anoint My head with oil." He was comparing Simon and an unknown woman. She had poured perfumed oil upon His feet and had continued kissing them, but Simon had done nothing. It was the social welcome for guests to anoint them with fragrant oils and greet them with the double kiss on the cheeks—as is still the practice in the East. Simon had been too casual and had shown Jesus no such respect.

The social anointing of guests was a cosmetic, not only imparting a pleasant smell to the guests but also helping their appearance by making their faces shine (Ps. 104:15). An oiled and shining face was considered admirable in those days. Cones of perfumed ointment were placed on the heads of guests so that when they became warm, the ointment would trickle down their faces and onto their clothes, pervading the atmosphere with a pleasant odor. Jesus accepted it from this woman who lavished on Him the best that money could buy.

Mary also anointed Jesus. Her ointment was spikenard, described as a very precious, rare preparation of nard brought from northern India at immense expense and prepared with the almost secret art of the perfumer. Sold in long-necked alabaster containers, it kept for years—it would even improve in quality and value. Many of these containers have been found on archaeological sites. Filled with ointment, they were kept as an investment, a household treasure.

The fragrance of Mary's oil was so rich that it pervaded the whole house. It was a tremendous sacrifice and an act of love's prodigal extravagance. It speaks of the love of God, through Jesus Christ, which brings us the priceless gift of the anointing of the Holy Spirit. It is no cheap experience; it's God's best.

The most common ingredient of cosmetic ointment was myrrh, refined from the sap that oozes from slits made in a small tree. We often read of it in Scripture. The girl loved by Solomon had fingers that dripped with sweet-smelling myrrh, and Solomon himself came from the dusty wilderness "perfumed with myrrh and frankincense" (Song of Sol. 3:6). Part of the beauty treatment for Esther for her presentation to King Ahasuerus was six months with oil of myrrh.

The value of it is shown when the Magi brought the infant Jesus myrrh as a special gift. People carried myrrh in their clothes. Taken medicinally, myrrh was used as an opiate, which is why Jesus refused it on the cross.

The idea of anointing oil originated in the pouring of ointment upon priests to ordain them for service. Theirs was a special anointing oil described in Exodus 30, used only for the Lord's tabernacle and priests. Kings were also anointed. Most commentaries say prophets were also anointed, but in fact not one of them ever was, because they were never appointed to be a prophet as if it were to an office, like priest or king. They were independent men of God, not socially appointed. God chose and gave them the real anointing with the Spirit. Nobody made prophets. They were God's men. By divine command Elijah should have anointed Elisha, but he failed to do so. God Himself anointed Elisha with the Spirit.

It was the habit to call the Spirit of God by the name of a prophet—the "spirit of Moses" or the "spirit of Elijah"—as a personal and rare distinction. The "spirit of Moses" was to be put upon the elders of Israel, and Elisha wanted a double portion of the "spirit of Elijah." The Spirit was identified with the prophet, and when God anoints believers today, it is with "the spirit of the prophets" or the "spirit of prophecy."

The true anointing is always by the Lord. Oils and precious ointments were emptied upon priests and kings as mere symbols or acknowledgments that God's Spirit had chosen to rest upon them. God was the originator, and such men were therefore called "the anointed of the Lord" or "the anointed of God"—especially Christ (Hebrew, *mashiyach*, which means "anointed" or "Messiah"), who is "the Christ (anointed) of God." Today among believers the anointing is a sovereign act of God.

Disciples and apostles were never anointed with oil. In the New Testament, Christians received the Holy Spirit for their work of service. Oil was never poured upon Jesus except by a woman for His burial, as I mentioned previously. Before the Day of Pentecost, priests were anointed and carried the fragrance with them, but since Pentecost believers carry the "Spirit of Christ." "They realized that they had been with Jesus" (Acts 4:13). The real had come.

Anointing with oil was retained in the New Testament only for the healing of the sick.

Our anointing flows out of Christ's anointing, and we

receive it only from Him. "Of His fullness we have all received" (John 1:16). To John the Baptist it was revealed that "upon whom you see the Spirit descending, and remaining on Him, this is He who baptizes with the Holy Spirit" (John 1:33). John identified the source—Jesus Christ, the giver and the authority of the giving.

We may pray and lay hands on people to be baptized in the Spirit, as the apostles did (Acts 8:17), but we must realize that a man cannot, and need not, give his anointing to someone else. The anointing comes out of Christ's fullness, not somebody else's fullness. I want my own anointing from God, not a secondhand anointing. To bestow "an anointing," even as a temporary effect, is foreign to Bible thought.

It comes "out of His fullness" as a constant outflow. Jesus alone is the baptizer. The blessings of God may flow in many ways through our lives as rivers of living water from Christ, but that is a very different thing from doing what only Jesus can do—impart the Spirit. The virgins refused to share their oil and were counted wise.

However, the word *anointing* today has acquired a broader meaning among believers. It is a word for general blessing. When people offer to bring us "an anointing" by laying their hands upon us, we need make no great objection. Scripturally there is no such thing as an anointing, only *the* anointing, but we need not be too strict about the use of a word, providing of course it does not convey a wrong piece of theology and that the exclusive sense of giving the Holy Spirit is not intended; it should only be a prayer for help, strength, guidance, and so forth.

I once, by nothing less than divine leading, found myself far from where I should have been, staring at a house in Clapham, London. A name plate outside referred to George Jeffreys, whom many consider to have been the greatest British revivalist since John Wesley. This man had filled the greatest halls and pioneered, in the face of universal opposition, the glorious message of Jesus Christ as Savior, healer, baptizer, and coming King. I could hardly believe it—I had just read one of this great man's books. Was he really there?

I dared to go and ask—and he heard my voice and invited me in. There he prayed with me, and it was as if his mantle had come upon me—to use a scriptural expression. God heard that man's prayer for me. I was already baptized in the Spirit—anointed—but sometimes we lack language to describe all that God does. I know that making contact with George Jeffreys and hearing his prayer for me was a special experience, which brought me a sense of equipping and readiness for service when I had just that day left the Bible college at Swansea to begin my full-time service for God. God had called me to His work, and now this special experience seemed to cover me.

David was anointed king by Samuel, from which David understood that he was the Lord's anointed. Later the elders of Israel also anointed him as their assurance of his call to them as king. "Anointings" are not to be expected every time we meet a special evangelist or teacher. For me it was one time only, after my call, when I met a man who had done the same work as God wanted me to do, like Elisha following Elijah.

Some experiences, which we may call anointings for lack of a better expression, may come as the assurance of God to a particular call, like that to Elisha or of the elders of Israel to David. To some they have come when listening to some other man of God, when they knew God was thrusting them forward as what Paul calls "the more honorable" members of the body of Christ.

George Canty, my cowriter, had been put off by the methods of some healing evangelists and was critical of such activity. God had been pressuring him for some time, asking him, "Where are all your mighty miracles?" One day he sat listening as a healing evangelist rose to speak. As soon as the man quoted his text, George Canty felt a sudden spiritual elevation to a new plane and knew that he would do what the preacher had done—heal sick people. The impression was so vivid that he had to look around to assure himself that the building was real, because it seemed such a vision-like and transcendent moment. He knew he was different.

Anointing and appointing go together. As I mentioned previously, the only people anointed were those selected for a particular task, especially that of priest or king. It was not a mere experience for emotional enjoyment. Nor did it signify that a special level of holiness had been attained. The anointing was given solely to equip and condition ordinary people to serve the Lord. The anointing was not available apart from service. Today the anointing is for all believers, for all are to serve. We are "a royal priesthood" (1 Pet. 2:9). Note carefully that anointing is not a kind of emotional pleasure, but it comes into activity when we serve. David did not feel anointed in any particular sense, but when he faced Goliath, he knew it. Samson became strong only when he went into action for God, and then the Spirit of God came upon him (as in Judges 14:6). A strong man does not feel his strength when sitting down; he feels it only when he exerts himself.

THE ANOINTED ONE

Now we will look at some other considerations. We should particularly remember that anointing is likened to perfume. Psalm 45:8 is often quoted to refer to Christ: "All your garments are scented with myrrh and aloes and cassia." Cassia came from the distant Far East. Israel probably obtained it in the wilderness from passing traders. It provided a distinctive fragrance associated only with the dwelling place of God and its priests—it evoked thoughts of God.

Scripture calls Jesus "the anointed One": "Peter answered and said 'You are the Christ, the Son of the living God'" (Matt. 16:16). Jesus is the Christ, the anointed One. He is as exclusively anointed as He was exclusively the Son of God.

Christ is from the Greek word *christos*, which has the same meaning as the Hebrew word for *Messiah*.

Everything denoted by the anointing of the tabernacle, priests, and kings is fulfilled in Jesus. Christ is our Priest-King. "Your robes are fragrant…" (Ps. 45:8, NIV). He carried the purity and odor of heaven, that evocative and subtle beauty of spirit that makes Him the anointed One, distinguished from all others. He drew people, not merely by power or "charisma" in the popular sense, but by love, moving in the atmosphere of His own holiness, which people had never breathed before. If we can put it this way, Jesus was God's alabaster box, broken for us on the Cross and now filling the world with His fragrance.

Personal beauty is never condemned in Scripture. Pride, lack of modesty, provocative dress, and flirtation certainly are. God makes people beautiful and does not expect us to belong to the cult of ugliness and make the worst of ourselves. The "saints" of the early centuries boasted of the population of lice in their hair and beards. Nuns were proud that water never touched their feet except when they crossed a river. God does not take special delight in the quaint, dowdy, or drab. He creates what will delight us, from the glory of the dawn to the majesty of sunset and the spangled velvet of the night sky. His dwelling is the light of setting suns. Our very means and genius to create beauty come from Him. Scripture says He "has made everything beautiful in its time"

(Eccles. 3:11). "Let the beauty of the LORD our God be upon us" (Ps. 90:17). That is what the anointing is.

"The beauty of holiness" forbids pride. Pride is the "dead flies," which "putrefy the perfumer's ointment, and cause it to give off a foul odor" (Eccles. 10:1). Our proud efforts at "holiness" are described in Isaiah 64:6: "All our righteousnesses are like filthy rags." That is because they produce a censorious and condemnatory attitude against those whom we suppose to have lower standards; it's an unattractive, narrow, and negative correctness while putting on spiritual airs and graces. In a legalistic life there is no more soil for true fruit of the Spirit than for orchids on arctic ice.

GIFTS OR THE GIVER

It is absolutely necessary to understand that the Holy Spirit is He, not "it." The Spirit is not an impersonal force, a sort of spiritual electricity. The anointing of God is not just power or gifts but the Holy Spirit Himself.

When people first stepped into modern history, speaking with tongues, they were called "the tongues people."[2] In fact, the memory of those people is still among us, and they carried an impressive godliness whose motive was service, not sensation; the Giver not the gifts. They longed to know Jesus better and to be more Christlike, not simply to have power for the sake of power. Their daily desire was to "let this mind be in you which was also in Christ Jesus, who...made Himself of no reputation, taking the form of a bondservant...and became obedient" (Phil. 2:5–8). Many laid down their lives for God.

When Jesus healed the sick, it was not just sheer voltage power He wielded, but it was also the power of His conquering love. He healed the sick by His stripes—that was the secret wonder of His anointing. He healed a withered arm, although it provoked men to plot against His life. He risked everything and would go to any lengths, even to a Roman cross, for the sake of the suffering.

Pain and the ministry of healing are strangely linked. When some of us are willing to know "the fellowship of His sufferings" (Phil. 3:10) and feel the same anointing of love that Jesus had and the same heartbreaking pity that forgets self and that will make any sacrifice for the afflicted, as Jesus did...when we become so identified with the sufferer that we would share suffering to ease others' pain, as Jesus did, and are "touched with the feeling of [their] infirmities" (Heb. 4:15, KJV) and afflicted in all their afflictions, as Jesus was...then perhaps fewer people would go home unhealed. I know of no profanity worse than healing the sick in Jesus's name in order to get rich, or to make a name for oneself, or for the gratification of wielding power.

A NEW ANOINTING?

We have already explained that God never anointed anybody twice. David was anointed of the Lord through Samuel; later Israel's elders did anoint him a second time, but that was confirming their acceptance of his kingly authority. The anointing through Samuel was a divine anointing. Jesus was anointed by God. Afterward a woman poured ointment on Him, which He said was for His burial. Normally priests and kings had only one anointing, and that was at the beginning of their career.

Some sing "Oh, for a new anointing" and pray for "another Pentecost," but the whole concept of another and new anointing, as if the original anointing had faded away, is strange to New Testament thought of the eternal Spirit. The anointing is self-renewing—it renews us, not we it. He is the Spirit of newness. First John 2:27 says, "The anointing which you have received from Him abides in you." Exodus 40:15 says, "You shall anoint them...that they may minister to Me." Second Samuel 1:21 speaks of the "shield of the mighty" being anointed for battle, and Leviticus 6 tells us of the anointing for sanctified service and holiness.

We can pray with our hands laid upon our friends to bring God's strength and blessing, but we must not suppose we can "top up" a person with the Spirit each time, assuming the enduement has died away. The Holy Spirit does not evaporate! If we are doing the work to which God called us, the anointing rests upon us without ever becoming less. We receive it moment by moment, like a waterfall fed by a never-failing river. All that is usually necessary is that we release His energies by working in His name.

The anointing is not to make us as conspicuous as Joseph

in his coat of many colors. In a TV commercial a young lady with a very bad cold, who cannot smell, sprays herself with more and more perfume. When she opens the door to her admirer, her perfume overpowers him and knocks him down. It is human to want overwhelming power, to bring an impact that everybody can feel. John the Baptist wore conspicuous clothing, a rough garb, and ate peculiar food. This told everybody he was a holy prophet. Jesus did neither. He dressed inconspicuously and ate anything set before Him. Many were awed in the presence of Jesus, but it was not by that kind of magnetism. It came as concern and love for men and women—that is why they fell down and worshiped Him.

In ourselves, sinful and limited, we are utterly incapable, either by personal ability or holiness, of becoming the temples of the Spirit, but still we are His temples. We wonder and worship. When that mighty Spirit takes up His abode with us, then oil, hands, or anything else upon our outer flesh are tokens only of His indwelling greatness.

Along with anointing, as we said, there are other symbols of the Spirit, but we have especially looked at this one for a very good reason. What we are trying to teach in this book cannot be learned like studying for an examination, but it must enter the heart and flow out in life—it must "take root downward and bear fruit upward" (Isa. 37:31).

Paul wrote to the Philippians about the loveliness of Christ's humility; then he went on to mention two women who were at odds with each other, Syntyche and Euodis.

Then, with great tact, he first thanked the Philippians for their recent kindness and described it as "a sweet-smelling aroma"—in Greek, *euodia*, a gentle hint to Euodia herself (Phil. 4:18).

The inward Spirit is seen by outward effects, physical indications of an inward and spiritual cause. To hanker for mere power in order to show off is corrupting, odious, and not fragrant. The real power of God only comes with the Holy Spirit, who reveals the loveliness of the Christ life and His graciousness—"Love to the loveless shown, / That they might lovely be."[3]

CHAPTER 4

HOW THE
GIFTS CAME

OW WE TURN our attention to the whole question of how the gifts of the Spirit became available to us today. A little word of caution first. If there is one thing in which there have been innovations and novel methods, it is in receiving the Holy Spirit and His gifts. Some alignment to the Word of God is needed in this area. The gifts are not tricks, techniques, or abilities we can pick up by watching others. God is pouring out His Spirit, and He needs no imitation gifts.

It is not a matter of learning the correct approach and making an achievement of it. If they could be achieved, they would not be gifts. Gifts are for those in the kingdom of God—they belong there.

Israel's blessings are covenanted to the Commonwealth of Israel. Christ Jesus linked wonders to the new Christian commonwealth—"If I cast out demons with the finger of God, surely the kingdom of God has come upon you" (Luke 11:20).

The "finger of God" was the Holy Spirit, as Peter tells us: "God anointed Jesus of Nazareth with the Holy Spirit and with power, who went about...healing all who were oppressed by the devil" (Acts 10:38). There is no power greater than that of the Holy Spirit. That is kingdom power. By the Spirit God distributes His ministries to whom He chooses.

MIRACLES CHARACTERIZE THE KINGDOM

My assurance to all readers and learners is that miracles are normal for the kingdom. Christ sent His disciples out and said, "Whatever city you enter, and they receive you...heal the sick there, and say to them, 'The kingdom of God has come near to you'" (Luke 10:8–9). Until the time of Christ, miracles were rare, being special historic visitations of God, and were divinely initiated by His sovereign will.

There were no gifts of healings for the blind, crippled, or deaf. Outstanding people such as David, Ezra, Nehemiah, Jeremiah, and Esther never once witnessed a physical wonder, and some never witnessed anything they could call supernatural. Ezra never saw a vision or heard a call or a voice. He was not a prophet, nor did he feel the moving of the Spirit. He could only trust the Word alone. Generally the few signs and wonders that were seen were demonstrations to teach rulers, such as the despotic lords of Egypt, Babylon, and Israel. These wonders were designed to humble them, as it did Nebuchadnezzar. He was forced to admit that "His [God's] dominion is an everlasting dominion, and His kingdom is from generation to generation.... I, Nebuchadnezzar, praise and extol and honor the King of heaven" (Dan. 4:34, 37).

Usually such events as the plagues of Egypt were judgments. John the Baptist, the last of the Old Testament prophets, expected that kind of judgment when the Messiah came. But the higher marks of kingdom power are kindness and mercy. John spoke of the fire cleansing and burning up the chaff, but when Jesus baptizes with fire, it does not bring destruction or judgment, but it brings a blaze of love. Jesus sent John the Baptist a message to show that His fire was His rage against the evils that men suffered. He was the One who should come. The gifts of the Spirit are benevolent and kind.

The same kind of contrast that was between John and Jesus is seen between Elijah and Elisha. Elijah was a prophet of fire and judgment; his successor was a prophet of kingdom mercies.

When Jesus met a blind man, He said, "I must work the works of Him who sent me while it is day" (John 9:4). By this he showed that the restoration of the blind was His Father's work. Kingdom mercies continued as long as Jesus was in the world, and they subsequently resumed after He had gone. In that same verse Jesus told His disciples, "The night is coming when no one can work." He meant that soon He would be crucified, night would fall, and there would be no blind receiving their sight. He also said to the disciples, "Without Me you can do nothing" (John 15:5). Neither did they for a time. Then came what Jesus had promised them— power, when the Holy Spirit came.

POWER BY BAPTISM
IN THE SPIRIT

Now if the power of the kingdom is the Holy Spirit, then kingdom power was given to the church on the Day of Pentecost. It is more than power and authority. In a saying of key importance Christ announced to His followers, "It is your Father's good pleasure to give you the kingdom" (Luke 12:32).

Believers inherit the kingdom "lock, stock, and barrel." The kingdom power, which rested on Christ Jesus, was there in order to work signs and wonders. The same Spirit is given to those within the kingdom of God for the same kingdom purposes. As John the Baptist revealed, "Upon whom you see the Spirit descending, and remaining on Him, this is He who baptizes with the Holy Spirit" (John 1:33). The Spirit, who endowed Jesus, now endows His people with the same power.

There is a difference between Christ and His followers, and it is rather noticeable! The difference is first Himself—who He is. Those who say, "The words of Christ on our lips are the same as those on Christ's lips," must remember this: it is not the words that matter but who says them. We may be adopted sons of God, but Jesus is the eternal and only begotten Son of God. The second difference is that the Spirit comes from Him. He is the source. We are not sources but channels, riverbeds through which the waters of His fullness flow.

Until Christ, nobody had been baptized in the Spirit. The term means something different from the attachment of the Spirit to Old Testament men and women. First Samuel 16:13 says Samuel took the horn of oil and anointed David, and the Spirit of the Lord "came upon David from that day forward." Such experiences are never expressed as a "baptism." The Holy Spirit's relationship with blood-washed, born-again believers is new. John 14:17 says that the Spirit "dwells with you and will be in you." That is why a new expression is used. It is to express a new kind of experience.

PARAKLETOS

People under the old covenant knew nothing of speaking with tongues, casting out demons, and healing by the laying on of hands (Mark 16:17–18). These signs were reserved for the age of the Spirit. A new kingdom, a new covenant, new features, and a new gospel for spirit and body describe the Christian age. Jesus used a new word for the Holy Spirit, *parakletos*, used five times in John's Gospel. It is translated "Comforter" (kjv) and "Helper." It belongs to the Greek word *parakaleo*, which means to call for somebody, to enlist their sympathy.

Think about the promise of "another Helper." To understand, we need only emphasize the word *another*. Jesus had been the *parakletos* to His disciples and had said to them, "I will not leave you orphans" (John 14:18). Jesus regularly used only one word for God—Father. For those who are in Christ Jesus, that one word also describes their relationship to almighty God. So when Jesus gave His last assurances to His disciples, He told them to "wait for the Promise of the Father.... 'you shall be baptized with the Holy Spirit'" (Acts 1:4–5). Also, He related the gift of the Spirit to the Father in Luke 11:13: "How much more will your heavenly Father give the Holy Spirit to those who ask Him!" If we were orphans, we would not receive the Spirit. Those who are "led by the Spirit of God, these are sons of God" (Rom. 8:14).

A quite breathtaking view of the kingdom is shown us in John 14:12: "He who believes in Me, the works that I do he will do also; and greater works than these he will do, because I go to My Father." (The word for "greater," *meizon*, does not specify what order of greatness, whether in number, quality, or magnitude.) This has been a problem to many Bible students. Surely nothing could outclass the miracles of Jesus in intrinsic omnipotence, such as the raising of Lazarus?

There are two senses in which someone can do "greater" things than Christ. Obviously there are some works of His that we could never do, since He is the Son of God. He is the Redeemer. Only He could die for the sins of the whole world. The works to which He referred were works of mercy, deliverance, healing, and aid. First there could be more numerous instances, and second, these could be spread over a wider area. Both took place, as the disciples moved out in missionary travel.

For centuries, since the invention of printing and now modern technology, far more vast operations can bring results, which were impossible to Jesus when He was localized in this or that village or town. He was physically limited, but He was not limited in power. He needed more hands, more voices, as extensions to Himself, and so "we are members of His body" (Eph. 5:30). The hymnwriter expresses it this way: "The arms of love that compass me / Would all the world embrace." [1] They are our arms, but they are also His.

This could only be through the power of the Spirit. Jesus emphatically repeated this:

> Most assuredly, I say to you, he who believes in Me, the works that I do he will do also; and greater works than these he will do, because I go to My Father....It is to your advantage [Greek: *sumphero*, "be expedient, be advantageous"] that I go away; for if I do not go away, the Helper will not come to you.
>
> —JOHN 14:12; 16:7

This is our basis for the gifts of the Spirit.

THE WORLD
BURSTS INTO VIEW

Reading the Bible from the beginning, we find ourselves concerned only about Israel—book after book, as if God was only the God of the Jews and had limited His interests to that tiny land and small nation. But as soon as we open the New Testament, the borders melt away and the wide world comes into view. True Jesus did say (for His own ministry), "I was not sent except to the lost sheep of the house of Israel" (Matt. 15:24), yet on that very occasion He restored a girl who did not belong to Israel but to a foreign nation. When He was in the synagogue at Nazareth, he also spoke of Elijah's dealings with the widow of Zarephath (Luke 4:25–27). His statement against racial discrimination infuriated the congregation, but He went to that non-Israel area later.

After Christ rose from the dead, the disciples retained a Jewish outlook for a long time and saw their new faith as belonging only to Israel. They even asked the Lord, an hour or so, before He ascended, "Lord, will You at this time restore the kingdom of Israel?" And He said to them, "It is not for you to know times or seasons, which the Father has put in His own authority. But you shall receive power when the Holy Spirit has come upon you; and you shall be witnesses to Me in Jerusalem, and in all Judea and Samaria, and to the end of the earth" (Acts 1:6–8). When the Holy Spirit fell, the disciples spoke with the tongues of people from many distant countries, displaying the ethnic interests of the Holy Spirit. What God did at Babel, scattering the people by confounding their languages, He reversed at Pentecost, uniting them by different languages.

KINGDOM SECRET

The gospel that the disciples preached as they went out was the gospel of the kingdom of God—the good news that the kingdom was close at hand. But they preached it in terms not used by John the Baptist and only sometimes by Jesus Himself. Their kingdom gospel was in the language of Christ crucified. It was not a different gospel, but it contained a tremendous new, vital fact about the kingdom—the Cross. When Jesus had spoken of it earlier, Peter had even tried to rebuke Him (Matt. 16:22). What seemed outrageous to the disciples at that time, they later realized was the all-important mystery of the kingdom, the self-sacrifice of the King for the kingdom.

The kingdom was established by the titanic battle and victory of Christ. His blood marks its foundations. Calvary is the source of the redemptive dynamic of God, the nuclear power-drive of the gospel, and of all the gifts of the Spirit.

For those moving into a real charismatic relationship, we are obliged to mention that modern religionists are busy building Calvary bypasses. Roads that avoid Calvary prove to go nowhere. There are no circuitous routes. The kingdom of God has a checkpoint and border control, and it is at the

Cross. Without having been to Calvary, everybody lives a second-class existence as illegal immigrants. Passport and entry permits are repentance and faith in Christ Jesus. Then we may enter the kingdom with the full privileges of citizens, "no longer strangers and foreigners, but fellow citizens with the saints and members of the household of God" (Eph. 2:19). The covenants of promise are ours.

We are not beggars asking the glorified saints to send us a few scraps of help. We do not need to collect their bones, hoping that some of their holiness or grace will brush off on us and stand to our credit. Believers are not bone pickers. If we do what the apostles did, we shall get what the apostles got from the same Father by the same Spirit on the same terms of grace.

The gifts are given to us freely. There are cheapjack imitations on the market, religious novelties, vibrations, spirit powers, healing sunbeams, and sweetness and light from nowhere in particular. In many countries our work disturbs those who have their own claims to power, protection, and healing.

I recall a especially powerful witch being brought over from America specifically to cast a spell and destroy what I was preaching. She stood at the back of the crowd and went through her performance. I wore the whole armor of God, and as she attempted to speed the harmful spirit-spear at me across the field, it turned back upon her. Her attempt was futile against a blood-bought child of God.

But the Holy Spirit waits at the Cross, and those who kneel at that altar, and there alone, receive His limitless blessings. At Calvary are benefits far beyond the labored results of mantras, New Age processes, and occultism. These are "the weak and beggarly elements" that Paul described in Galatians 4:8–11.

How real and how great His gifts are we shall see.

CHAPTER 5

GOLDEN RULES
OF THE GIFTS

MY PURPOSE IN writing this book is not a wish to intrigue readers but to emphasize that the gifts have a vital part to play in world evangelism. They are weapons of war, not toys to be played with. Mark 16 firmly anchors miracles to the Great Commission.

From the outset the church looked doomed, stillborn. To bring His message to the nations Jesus had only a few ordinary men from Galilee. None of them showed any brilliance or personal qualities that would make for success, and they displayed a generous share of human failings. They were as unqualified as world conquerors as men ever could be. The Jewish leaders wrote them off as ignorant and unlearned. Their message should have appealed to nobody. It had no element of intellectual wisdom, political promise, or immediate social benefit. Its worst disqualification for popular acceptance was that it was centered on a leader from a seedy Galilean backwater who had been executed as a common criminal.

Mission impossible? Against all expectations it became "mission accomplished." How? These nobodies advanced with a new secret. God personally worked with them with signs and wonders. More than that, He barbed their simple words with conviction and guided them to the hearts of hearers as unerringly and powerfully as David's stone to the head of Goliath. Without personal charisma, the charisma of the Spirit of God endued them. Their "secret"? The Holy Spirit.

Let us take it from there. If Christianity is to progress, this is the divine way. Christ knew that the world would expand. There are now sixty times more people alive than when He was here. He expected that all the world would hear His quiet words spoken so long ago in an obscure Roman province—not by normal propaganda methods but by His power.

Because the world hovers between spiritual life and death, the utmost consideration must be given to whatever can secure the destinies of precious people. What follows are principles of real importance. They may even be stressed by repeated mention throughout following chapters.

Just as in the wilderness Jesus was tempted to misuse divine powers when He had been filled with the Holy Spirit, so are others likely to be.

The core of the test is our pride, which corrupts our sincere motives for the power gifts and produces flamboyant behavior and egotistic display. Jesus was tempted by the devil to throw Himself off the temple pinnacle. One thing to be taken to heart is that the supernatural is not always sensational. We can attract personal admiration by our gifts, but our job is to set people's eyes on Jesus. When Paul and Barnabas were offered worship at Lystra, they were horrified, running among the people to assert they were not divinities (Acts 14:8–18).

"This generation seeks a sign," said Jesus (Luke 11:29). Sensation always has a market. We can exploit that situation and turn the gifts of God to self-advantage. Simon Magus wanted the Holy Spirit, but only to bolster his prestige (Acts 8:9). Uzza died for his presumption in putting his hand upon the ark of testimony (1 Chron. 13:10). If anyone says, "I would like the gift of healing," or any gift, the proper reply is, "Why?" Motive is vital.

THE GIFTS OF THE SPIRIT DO NOT CONFIRM ANYBODY'S METHODS OR THEOLOGY

The gifts operate by faith in God, not faith in a specific theory. They are not channeled through any doctrine except that of redemption. The Holy Spirit only glorifies the crucified Christ. Testimonies that this or that formula has brought success are always to be found, but they do not prove what they are supposed to prove. God's mercies are "broader than the measures of our mind."[1] There is only one secret—faith. "This is the victory...our faith" (1 John 5:4). New techniques and highly publicized methods may seem to bring results, but they do not. God separates the techniques from the faith and responds only to faith.

In the New Testament, whenever healings and miracles are attributed to anything at all, it is invariably to faith. Otherwise it is the sovereign action of God. "Thy faith hath made thee whole; go in peace," Jesus said to the woman with a hemorrhage (Luke 8:48, KJV). Her "method" could not have been more simple and childlike. Those seeking healing can be helped by teaching, but the essential miracle ingredient is still simple, trusting faith in Jesus. That is all God bothers about, no matter what notions or innovations occupy our sometimes muddled brains.

GIFTS COME WITH OPPORTUNITY

They are issued to workers as they clock in at the door. Like modern technology, God's work needs specialized equipment, but it is found "on the job." He does not hand it to us to keep handy in case we can use it sometime somewhere.

The need of the healing gift arises when we are moved by the plight of sufferers. That is when the gift operates. Jesus was moved with compassion. The word means physically churned up and shocked. When your stomach turns over and you have to blink tears away at the sight of people, miserable and depressed with afflictions and ailments, and you feel like screaming in protest at their condition—go ahead; God will give all you need.

GIFTS DO NOT COME SECONDHAND

It is solely the prerogative of the Spirit to bestow them. Many have presumed to give "gifts" to other believers, but mainly it has led to disappointment—miracle powers have not followed. We have not heard of any outstanding ministry produced by such attempts at transference.

I would like to give some guidance on meetings held to "teach" gifts. Teaching about gifts is good, but to receive gifts purely by being taught how to do things is no more possible than to acquire a musical or artistic gift by learning.

However, where there is faith and true desire in our heart, a true gift may be bestowed by the Spirit at any time, so it may happen, not surprisingly, where people are listening eagerly to explanations about the *charismata*. But it is by the will of the Holy Spirit, not man's will. Be assured that, while the Spirit completely ignores the pretentious "giftings" of the will of men, He does not ignore true openness and prayer. We can pray humbly for one another that we may be equipped for the work. Paul himself asked for prayer that he might open his mouth boldly because the door of opportunity was there (1 Cor. 16:9; Eph. 6:19; Col. 4:3). The point to learn in those verses is that when the opportunity arose, Paul sought prayer help from everybody.

Perhaps we should take a few minutes to examine scriptures that have been offered as grounds for "giftings." As a preliminary, we mention the fact that no scripture is ever claimed to exist that gives instructions or commands for the practice. There are at best no more than oblique inferences.

Romans 1:11 says, "I long to see you, that I may impart to you some spiritual gift [*charisma*], so that you may be established." What is that charisma? He tells us—"that is, that I may be encouraged together with you by the mutual faith both of you and me" (v. 12). "This verse does not apply," says Dr. S. Schatzmann in "A Pauline Theology of Charismata," "for it has not the same technical sense of 'gift' as in 1 Corinthians 12."[2] It must be taken in context. Many *charismata* (gifts) are mentioned by Paul that are not miraculous endowments for believers. Indeed, the whole Christian faith consists of *charismata*, from salvation to sanctification.

However, it is quite clear that Paul in Romans 1:11 is not thinking of giving an individual a "gift," for he is addressing the whole body of believers at Rome. He was not traveling all the way to Rome to bestow a gift of wisdom or discernment upon one man or woman but, as he says, to "establish" the whole church.

Other scriptures are 1 Timothy 4:14 and 2 Timothy 1:6. Paul told Timothy "do not neglect" and "to stir up" the gift (*charisma*) given him by the laying on of Paul's hands and that of the eldership. Was this a "gift" as in 1 Corinthians 12:8–10? If so, how could he "stir it up"? However, we are actually told what this gifting was, namely "a spirit of power, not timidity, and of love and self-discipline" (See 2 Timothy

1:7, NIV.) The "gifting" by the elders was for his general ministry as a young Christian worker.

GOD GIVES WHATEVER WE NEED WHEN WE OBEY HIS CALL TO SERVICE

When Timothy was thrust into a difficult task, Paul prayed and laid hands upon him with other elders, and God blessed Timothy for the work, a normal procedure. A similar situation is found in Acts 13:1–3. The church at Antioch laid hands on Paul and Silas to "separate" them for the work to which God had already called them. No "gifting" was attempted, but the laying on of hands was more than a ritual—it identified a need for strength from God. One can hardly suppose anybody would choose one "gift" of the nine for a young fellow left alone in a pagan world with a small company of believers, as if it were a going-away present. I cannot imagine which one Paul and the elders would choose for the big task that lay ahead of Timothy, but a general pastoral gifting—yes.

Another scripture quoted for "gifting" is the passage in 2 Kings 2, where Elisha asked Elijah to give him a double portion of his spirit. Elijah said it was a hard thing but promised it would be so if Elisha saw Elijah taken away (v. 10). There are several points to note here.

God had already called Elisha to take the place of Elijah. He was his spiritual heir. This is what is meant when Elisha asked for "a double portion of your spirit." This did not mean twice as much power, though he did work twice as many miracles as Elijah. A "double portion" was the elder son's share of an inheritance (Deut. 21:17). Elijah was Elisha's spiritual father.

When the call of God already rests upon a man's soul, which was the case with Elisha (1 Kings 19:16), then, when an Elijah passes from the scene, God lets the same mantle fall on other shoulders. It is of God when such men come together. It has happened again and again.

These are the main scriptures used for "gifting" (as practiced originally by the Latter Rain movement of the 1940s and 1950s). The Holy Spirit is not directed by Christians. He directs Christians. We must not usurp the sovereign prerogatives of almighty God. The definitive New Testament chapters concerning spiritual gifts—1 Corinthians 12–14—tell us to desire gifts, especially to prophesy, but they never suggest that gifts can be conferred by one person upon another, as we would expect if that was how God meant it to be.

Instead the stress is laid on people "desiring" (1 Cor. 14:1), "seeking" (v. 12), and "praying" (v. 13), but never that one should pray for another to receive. What is stated in 1 Corinthians 12:11 is that the Spirit apportions "to each one individually as He wills."

The Holy Spirit does not wait for the church to take the initiative as to who should be gifted. The Lord has not committed Himself to empower those whom the church appoints. If a church must choose, then the New Testament model is for men already full of faith and the Holy Spirit (Acts 6:3, 5) to be chosen. Obviously God does not use unsuitable personalities, like warriors to be nursemaids or musicians to clean bricks, but God often has His own ideas as to what He can do with people. He does not wait to see how church ballots go.

Church leaders should have the eye of discernment for the God-gifted and should encourage them, giving them the place they are fitted for. Too often jealousy has arisen at the gifts of others, and rather than opportunity being given them, they have been ignored and left to do other work. To the eternal credit of the leaders at Antioch, there was no jealousy, and they released Paul into his world-shaping mission work.

The Bible never calls natural abilities "*charismata.*" Art, music, poetry, business acumen, linguistics, physical beauty, and intellectual strength are all assets that can be offered to God. Our skills may be enhanced in God's service, but they still remain abilities, not *charismata*. The true *charismata* are the gifts of the Spirit, which can be given even to those who are disadvantaged from birth.

Unfortunately too often churches and movements hold "men's persons in admiration" (Jude 16, KJV) if they look good, have the right accent and, as James 2:2 says, wear a gold ring and fine clothes. Samuel, sent to anoint a new king, looked admiringly on the impressive stature and personality of all Jesse's sons except David, the youngest, who was tending the sheep. He did not have the right-shaped head for a crown, nor did he have a hand for a scepter, but only a shepherd's staff. Yet of this fresh-faced youngster God said, "He is a man after my own heart."

We discover our gifts best in operation. The advice "find your gift and use it" may have some wisdom in it, for to hide one's abilities is neglect. Sloth may be disguised as humility. The parable of the talents recognizes no excuse. Unused capacities must be uncovered and recovered.

However, Scripture has better advice—beyond finding one's gift. Paul said, "I can do all things through Christ who strengthens me" (Phil. 4:13). "Find your gift" can be an excuse for doing nothing. Many say, "I have no gift." The truly "gifted" are those with no natural abilities but who are prepared to "get up and go." The soldier brothers of David mocked him, suggesting that he was no figure for the battle-field—keeping sheep was his lot. But his faith and anointing overcame all inexperience and deficiencies. God teaches a man to fight who does fight.

For the scriptural principle we turn to 1 Samuel 10:6–7: "The Spirit of the LORD will come upon you, and you will...be turned into another man....do as the occasion demands; for God is with you."

Chapters 12 and 14 of 1 Corinthians pivot on the central passage of love in chapter 13. Scholars say that the key words of this Corinthian epistle are *word* and *deed*, but in fact it is the word *love*. Paul's love touches every word and every deed in the epistle. A critical theologian has tried to show that Paul was recommending his own love merits in that chapter.[3] Perhaps he was, but why not? He is supposed to be an example, and indeed he is.

The gifts are not exclusively for the perfect, despite what is said in the previous section. Who is the perfect Christian? Life is a continuing demonstration of our inconsistent efforts to reach perfection. But the gifts are *charismata*—the favors of grace, not certificates of merit. The Book of Numbers is perhaps the prime Bible lesson in that subject, in which Israel is exhibited for its failures. The children of Israel all failed, sometimes grossly, including the noble triad of Moses, Aaron, and Miriam, as well as Aaron's sons. Then turn to the strange episode of Balaam. When he tried to curse Israel, he could not. He found out why when God allowed him to see Israel as He saw them. Balaam then declared, "He has not observed iniquity in Jacob, nor has He seen wickedness in Israel" (Num. 23:21).

Is there a price to pay for the gifts? If there is, they would not be gifts but purchases. Nevertheless, there well may be a price to pay in their use. Those not prepared to risk their leisure, their comfort, their reputation, and perhaps much more may be little used by God—even if He does bestow His power gifts upon them. A complete tool kit may be a marvelous gift for a carpenter, but it would be useless without the sweat of his brow. Gifts call for commitment; as Romans 12:7 puts it, "Let us use it in our ministering." His life is poured out with ours. Gifts are for givers. To get, give!

The value of any gift depends on the situation. A monkey

wrench in the garden is of far less use than a lawn mower. The power to heal is of little value among the young and healthy, but discernment would be. It has been suggested that Paul names the gifts in a descending order of value, but this is not supported by Scripture. In fact, gifts that come first in the original list are not named at all in the next list in the same chapter. Then again, Paul especially encourages the Corinthians to seek prophecy, but it is only sixth in the second list.

The gift lists do not mention every gift. Some, mentioned elsewhere, are omitted. For example, the casting out of demons is not mentioned in these lists. This suggests that there are other possibilities in the Holy Spirit. The idea that we must have a prior scriptural instance for every manifestation is itself not a biblical principle. No such idea is mentioned, otherwise what is the purpose of the instruction "test the spirits" (1 John 4:1)? There is a vast range of supernatural phenomena, and God does not tie Himself down to precedent.

Let me specify. Strange things took place in the classical revivals that are not found in the New Testament. Yet they are never questioned but are always taken as strong evidences of God at work. For that matter, classical revival itself has no parallel in Scripture. The Holy Spirit has never tied Himself down, nor should we assume that those revivals are the way He will always work. He never works contrary to the Bible, of course. For example, there may be minimum scriptural examples of believers being "slain in the Spirit," as some call it, though through the centuries it has been seen as an act of God. It does not contradict any revelation about the activity of God. Of course like the Egyptian sorcerers with Moses, what God does can be counterfeited and simulated, but that does not invalidate what is genuine.

The guidance of Paul in Corinthians regarding the gifts is not to be taken as the law of Mount Sinai. For example, verses 27 and 29 of 1 Corinthians 14 say, "If anyone speaks in a tongue, let there be two or at the most three, each in turn, and let one interpret.... Let two or three prophets speak, and let the others judge." These "imperatives" have been treated as law. Pastors have sternly rebuked a fourth utterance and declared it to be in the flesh and not of God. Half a church has been known to secede through the public humiliation of a sincere member making a fourth utterance. Presumably if the benediction had been first pronounced, and a second meeting begun, the tongues five minutes later would have been in order! Damage done by a graceless legal ruling is far beyond any damage that a fourth message can imaginably do.

If the whole of Paul's teaching is taken to heart, that kind of legalism would be impossible. All his rulings, whether on the gifts or on anything else, must be seen in a framework of grace. We are, of course, to take all Bible moral law with utter seriousness. The gifts are another matter; they spring from life in the Spirit, a lively, powerful, manifesting activity. To box in with cast-iron regulations the bubbling dynamic of the Spirit is insensitive and incompatible with the free energies of the Spirit.

Two thousand years ago, Paul was faced with the runaway exuberance and lack of wisdom from those who had just come out of heathenism and had little Christian experience, or even written Scripture to guide them. How can we today be "led of the Spirit" while the whip of law is cracked behind us? "Where the Spirit of the Lord is, there is liberty" (2 Cor. 3:17). These principles will reappear as we proceed with this comprehensive examination.

CHAPTER 6

WORDS OF THE WORD

E VERY SUBJECT HAS to have its special words, its own jargon, in order to avoid repetition. I know that people want a simple gospel, but to "grow in the grace and knowledge of our Lord and Savior Jesus Christ" (2 Pet. 3:18) without learning anything is impossible. Jesus said, "If you abide in Me, and My words abide in you, you will ask for what you desire, and it shall be done for you" (John 15:7). There are two vital conditions for prayer—abiding in Christ and His words abiding in us. To grasp the Bible meaning of this is important. The Bible makes the rules for studying the Bible. We will follow that principle now.

We begin with an expression mentioned frequently in this book: "spiritual." To describe somebody as "very spiritual" tells us a lot about them. Some Corinthians called themselves spiritual, but they did not mean what we mean, nor did they mean what Paul meant either. Paul was doubtful of them, as he shows in 1 Corinthians 14:37: "If anyone thinks himself to be...spiritual." These "spiritual men" had perhaps been associated with the mystery religions. Many claimed a secret and esoteric experience or had been "initiated." They were spiritual in the pagan or occult sense.

Paul gave "spiritual" a Christian meaning—a person filled with the Holy Spirit and walking in obedience and righteousness, not in the pride and lusts of the flesh. He refers to true and false spirituality in 1 Corinthians 12:1–7, and one of the tests there is that true spirituality produces something for "the profit of all" (v. 7). That is a principle that applies to all the gifts.

SPIRITUAL GIFTS

It was Paul's idea to talk about spiritual gifts. The Corinthians had not asked Paul because they thought they knew all that was to be known, but it did not leave Paul very happy. In 1 Corinthians 12:1 he said, "Now concerning spiritual gifts, brethren, I do not want you to be ignorant," which he judged they were. In 1 Corinthians 14:38 he says, "If anyone is ignorant, let him be ignorant." He meant that if they still thought that they knew it all and did not accept correction of their ideas, then they would stay ignorant. They had been "carried away" with their previous knowledge, which was similar, but belonged to "dumb idols" (1 Cor. 12:2). The Greeks were famous for worldly learning, but the things of the Spirit are different. A university doctorate in social sciences or physics does not make us wise in the things of God. These latter are learned by getting fire into one's soul, not just cold facts into one's head.

This is our major subject, so we will have a closer look at what they are called. First, we should know that chapter 12 of 1 Corinthians is really about the church. The teaching on spiritual gifts is incidental.

The Corinthians had written to Paul asking for help, and he had dealt with several matters that worried them. Sadly, some things that they should have worried about did not trouble them. They had allowed factions to divide the fellowship in Corinth, and that to Paul was a very alarming situation. Then also they had misused the gifts. Paul now points out these matters and relates both problems together. The result is this truly marvelous exposition that he has left us.

Our English versions use the phrase "spiritual gifts." Now, the original word in Greek really has nothing to do with "gift." It is *pneumatika* (from *pneuma*—spirit), which is found twenty-six times in the New Testament and is an adjective meaning "spiritual." In this specific context it is best understood as "concerning spiritual matters." This special word is translated "spiritual gift(s)" only three times, but mostly spiritual men, a spiritual law, meat, rock, body, songs, a house, and so on. In Romans 1:11 Paul wanted to impart a *pneumatikon* to the Romans, meaning "something spiritual," a benefit.

The proper word in Greek for "gift" is actually not used

in 1 Corinthians 12–14, except twice incidentally. The Corinthians liked the word *pneumatika*—it was their word, but Paul coined a special word, which he preferred—*charisma*. Once again he avoids the normal word for "gift" (*doron*) and chooses the word *charisma*, which is so well known today. It means "a favor." It is surprising that Paul does not use a straightforward "gift" word, but we shall see why.

Paul, the apostle of grace (*charis*), introduced this word into the Christian vocabulary. Grace is the free and unmerited favor of God and exemplifies God's benevolent attitude. The Old Testament talks about God turning His face toward us, showing the light of a favorable countenance. That is what grace really is—a kindly attitude—not a power, force, or substance. For long centuries the old theologians spoke as if grace were something measurable. Later, others thought of grace as a strange power that came upon people in an unpredictable way. They confused grace with the Holy Spirit. Even now many believe that there are saints who have accumulated large quantities of grace by their virtue—enough for themselves and for others, as a kind of spiritual coinage. The "means of grace" were the sacraments, by which people could gather grace to their credit account. But an abstract quality cannot be saved up.

However, the wonderful thing is, that although God's grace refers to His attitude, it is never abstract in Scripture. It always has a concrete form. Grace is His deeds and gifts. The only way we know His grace is by His practical demonstration of it. So "grace" has come to signify something tangible, good, and real. The greatest *charis* of all is Jesus Christ, "the indescribable gift." He is grace personified.

The sunshine and rain are acts of grace, for as Jesus said, "He makes his sun rise on the evil and on the good, and sends rain on the just and the unjust" (Matt. 5:45). God is the God of grace—that is His character, and that is the God with whom we have to do. Only on the grounds of His grace can we approach him. We earn nothing that He gives us—certainly not the spiritual gifts. Everything we have is a demonstration of His smiling goodness of heart toward us—food, sunshine, breath, and so on. Do not grumble about wet weather—the rain is a gift of God.

It is wonderful to know that grace itself is completely free. We do not have to seek favor with God by any kind of behavior that might impress Him. He loves us anyway. Grace is there all the time, like the air we breathe. Another lovely example of a real gift by grace is in Romans 5:15—"the gift by the grace," which means that grace is a real and permanent gift to us.

Nowadays, of course, everybody uses the word *charisma*. They talk about a "charismatic leader" or somebody with "charisma"—that is, with personality. It was introduced into modern language by Max Weber, a German professor, one of the founders of sociology in the last century. He turned it into his jargon word for leadership qualities. Leadership, however, is not what Paul was talking about.

There is still something else that we might be confused about. The gifts of the Spirit never designate natural talents such as a gift for music or art. They are our own abilities to use as we like, for good or evil. The gifts in 1 Corinthians 12 are supernatural manifestations of the Spirit. They only operate according to God's will, as the Spirit "gives utterance." Our will to use them depends on His will and His timing.

Before we go any further, I must explain why the gifts differ from person to person. Paul shows that there are all kinds of members with different gifts. He mentions a few of those gifts in the first list: miracles, healings, tongues, interpretation, and so on. Then later he brings in another order of gifts—people: apostles, prophets, teachers, helps, governments. These various classes of gifts are all *charismata* but different. Not everybody has the same part to play, yet all are equally important.

Paul speaks about the body having "less honorable" members (1 Cor. 12:23), which receive less admiration. He does not specify our "less honorable members" physically, but he does list some members of Christ who get little mention, particularly helps and governments. Feet do not get the same attention as faces. Paul adjusts that and places "helps" alongside the most eminent appointments, such as apostles, and on the same level as the mighty manifestations and gifts most highly valued by the Corinthians; i.e., tongues, interpretation, and miracles.

Paul is using the same principle as Jesus, who said, "He who receives a prophet in the name of a prophet shall receive a prophet's reward" (Matt. 10:41). Note, He did not say "in My name" but "in the name of a prophet." It means that to accept a prophet as a prophet, helping him, showing that you would do a prophet's work if you could, will bring you a reward equal to the prophet's reward. It is faithfulness in service that counts. One service does not outrank another. Christ became a servant to His servants and washed the disciples' feet, an act for which no supernatural powers are needed.

There is no such thing as greater and lesser gifts. A charisma is from God and therefore cannot be trivial. So many want to belittle tongues or despise them as no more than a peculiar psychological phenomenon or something arising from a deeper part of the mind that we cannot control. Those experiencing the tongues know that it is nothing of the kind, and they are the only ones who can judge. "He who is spiritual judges all things" (1 Cor. 2:15). Those—like the Corinthians—seeking the "best gifts" would do well to remember that we are never told to seek the best gifts. That is misreading the Word of God. All the *charismata* are favors of God and to be equally valued.

MANIFESTATION

"The manifestation of the Spirit is given to each one for the profit of all" (1 Cor. 12:7). The Greek word for "manifestation" comes from *phaneroo*, which means to show openly to be or to make manifest. The Holy Spirit shows Himself openly.

You will notice that in 1 Corinthians 12 Paul speaks mainly about the Holy Spirit Himself and the body of Christ. He is emphasizing who the Spirit really is and how we should distinguish the Holy Spirit from false spirits. He lists the gifts in order to show who is behind them—the "same Spirit" (v. 11). Whether it is tongues, interpretation, discernment, or anything else, it is the Holy Spirit showing Himself. God in action. In chapter 14, of course, he gives much more attention to the gifts. So "a word of knowledge" is a manifestation of the Spirit. That is what is given—a manifestation and not a permanent ability.

Speaking by the Spirit of God, nobody calls Jesus "accursed." Outside Christianity, ecstatic speech is demonic, and demons never glorify Jesus. There are different sources of supernatural phenomena. Spirits may manifest themselves and imitate the works and gifts of God.

Some have suggested that because speaking with tongues is heard among non-Christians, such as Spiritualists and Buddhists, all who speak with tongues are of the devil. It does not follow that if a Spiritualist speaks with tongues, then everybody who speaks with tongues is a Spiritualist. We may as well say that because burglars use a steel jimmy, everybody who uses a steel jimmy is a burglar. The fact that there is a counterfeit should not lead us to reject the genuine.

Wisdom, knowledge, healings, tongues, and so on are

manifestations, not gifts. They are actions of the Spirit, and an action cannot be a gift. The gift of music is not an action but an independent ability. The "gift," as we call it, simply means that a certain individual is often used by the Holy Spirit in a particular manner, such as prophecy or miracles. This will be clear when we look at each gift in turn.

"HOLY SPIRIT" AND "THE HOLY SPIRIT"

The Spirit behind these gifts is the same Spirit as in Genesis 1:2, who hovered over the face of the waters. Sometimes in the original texts we read of "the Holy Spirit," and sometimes just "Holy Spirit" without the definite article. Does this matter? Do we not sometimes speak of "the Holy Spirit" and sometimes of a "Holy Spirit meeting" or a "Holy Spirit gift?"

There is a difference, which it is really a blessing to understand. Whenever we read "the Holy Spirit," the Spirit Himself is referred to. It names Him as a person. When it is just "Holy Spirit," it is something He does, out of Himself, a manifestation. In Acts 2:17 we read that God will "pour out of [His] Spirit"—out of Him, some of Him. However, the wonderful thing to note is this: that what the Holy Spirit does is of Himself—He pours Himself out, and each gift is a manifestation of Himself. The power of the Spirit is the Spirit. We human beings cannot pour ourselves out. We can give our time or effort, but the Spirit Himself fills us. He is "given," an abiding gift, His presence within us. Jesus said,

"You shall receive power when the Holy Spirit has come upon you" (Acts 1:8). (See also 1 John 3:24; 4:13.)

His power is not an impersonal force that we can play with. Power is the Spirit, God in action, the same awesome personal force that created the heavens and the earth. To say to people, "Have some more Holy Spirit" or "I am giving you more anointing," is flippant. We cannot throw people a glass of God. The Spirit is not a spiritual stock-in-trade of evangelists or teachers to hand out as they fancy.

There is also no power of grace distinct from the Holy Spirit. The Holy Spirit is, Himself, a generating force. He generates us (John 3:3). We cannot generate power, for it is the Holy Spirit, and being the Holy Spirit, it cannot be generated by prayer, holiness, obedience, or any of the techniques and formulas now on the church market. God is not an energy that can be manufactured by using the right spiritual technique. To speak of getting twice as much power by twice as much prayer is a wrong idea. We are talking about a person. The power of God is channeled through the Word of God.

First Corinthians 12:4 says, "There are diversities of gifts, but the same Spirit." The word *diversities* is used for things widely different. Paul is drawing a sharp contrast between the variety of gifts and workings and the absolute single identity of the Holy Spirit. In the pagan temples and oracles of Paul's day, each separate god, such as Diana of the

Ephesians, had his or her temple, and the spirit of that god was supposed to operate there.

Some think that it does not matter and that all spirits belong to a common area of spirit, the spirit world. Outside the Christian faith, various religions have their techniques for tapping into the spirit world, some by mantras, some by spirit guides, and some by incantations or witchcraft practices, verbal formulas, magic words. The contemplatives and mystics tune in to the vibrations, voices, and forces to connect with this area of spirit. New Age takes in all manner of methods.

However God does not belong to any realm of spirit. He is above all gods, above all spirits. He is not to be compared with any spirit power. Buddhists, Zen, the Soka Gakkai, and many New Age cults claim to draw upon some mass force, such as cosmic power or the earth spirit.

Against all this the Bible brings the naked and searing light of truth—the truth that the Son of God, Jesus, by whose word all things were made, is above all principalities and powers and every name that can be named. He gives the Holy Spirit when we ask, without secret techniques or word power. There is no formula, only trust and love. Almighty God does not jump at our bidding to perform a mighty wonder, like some pet animal to a word of command.

Warnings in Scripture about counterfeit signs and wonders should be taken seriously. Satan has not retired from business (1 John 4:1). On the other hand, the genuine believer, trusting in Jesus Christ who shed His blood for us, is perfectly safe and need not fear that a scorpion spirit will be given him if he asks for the Holy Spirit (Luke 11:12). Believers are children of the kingdom. The first duty of a nation is the defense of the realm and the security of those within it. God is our salvation. We, in Christ, are dwellers in Zion, whose bulwarks and walls are impregnable. No marauding spirit can penetrate through to us. There is peace within its walls.

FOR THE COMMON GOOD

Almost the whole of 1 Corinthians 12 concerns the church, and the gifts are for the common good of all members. The church is Paul's ceaseless concern. He was the "steward of the mystery" of the church and of the amazing revelation of God's new creation, not built by getting like-minded people together but that which depends upon human differences, different gifts, and different people. Furthermore, in Christ, those differing personalities, created in Christ Jesus, are brought to the highest development of distinction yet in harmonious interplay.

The modern tendency is to depersonalize and reduce us to a few types. The world's idea is the club, a class of people with their mutual similarities and subtle marks. God's idea is the church. The first thing God does is break down these walls of partition and make each person a class on their own, a person in their own right. A body needs eyes, which are totally different from hair or nails. The church is the body of Christ and depends on the unlikeness of its members to complete it.

The great social and political schemes usually attempt to level us all, to put us all in some common class—all ants—or even to dress us all alike, as Chairman Mao's Chinese masses used to do. There is no cohesion unless each unit is molded to the same pattern, like bricks in a wall. God does not mold bricks but "living stones," as Peter writes in 1 Peter 2:5, each sculptured specially. The world sees distinctions as weakness, but God sees them as strength—weakness through uniformity, but strength through unity.

Spiritual gifts are supplemented by the gifts of apostles, prophets, evangelists, pastors, and teachers (Eph. 4:11), which are as different as chalk and cheese and yet brought together by divine chemistry creating together an indissoluble bond.

The whole book of 1 Corinthians is really about this unity. The Corinthians recognized differences, as between Paul, Peter, and Apollos. They attached themselves to one name or another, making them into cult figures. These groups vied with each other to be the main church party so that other members would join their cult figure faction. This attempt at sameness led to division. It was an ecumenical effort and it failed. Churches are supposed to be different, like the people in them, but all are one in Christ.

In the interest of ecumenical unity, whole denominations have compromised the very principles for which they existed and denied their history. Being different is no sin.

The expression "the profit of all" in 1 Corinthians 12:7 is the Greek word *sumphero*, from which comes the word *symphony*. The Holy Spirit is a composer conducting His own work, bringing counterpoint and harmony from many interlocking themes and instruments, not from everyone playing the same tune.

THE THREEFOLD WORK OF THE TRINITY

Having made ourselves familiar with some of the language about the Holy Spirit and the gifts, we will end this section with the words in 1 Corinthians 12:4–6:

> There are diversities of gifts, but the same Spirit. There are differences of ministries, but the same Lord. And there are diversities of activities, but it is the same God who works all in all.

Gifts, ministries, and activities, all different. Then it says "the same Spirit...Lord...God"—different names, but showing the same God. It is rather striking that when Paul is stressing that the same Spirit is behind the gifts, he uses three different names for God.

Why is that? It is to show again that the most perfect unity of all, that of the Godhead, embraces differences. Gifts by the Spirit, ministries by the Lord, activities by God. Three operations by three Persons in the Godhead, but one great work. The unity of the Spirit is complex. God is a complex Being—the Trinity. And so is the church. A pastor once joked, "It takes all sorts to make a world, and I've got them all in my church." Of course! Why not? I would like to unpack this text a little more.

Gifts

They are many (*charismata*).

Ministries

This implies eagerness or readiness to serve. The "blessed of My Father" in Matthew 25 did not know that they had served the Son of Man, Christ. What they had done was their heart's spontaneous outflow. Many people feel they are doing so little, that they have no ability, knowledge, or opportunity. But they stick to their church, and people like that make churches possible. What they do is what they are. The Holy Spirit is like that. He is what He is—alive, active, moving, concerned. Those whom He anoints find something within them moving them to serve; they are eager, full of zest, and faithful when they can do nothing.

Nobody should hold back or quench the Spirit by pretending to be humble and not wanting the limelight or by doing nothing until they "feel led"—or forced.

Some people seem not to "feel led" as often as they ought to be or as often as would help a church. Too many people not "feeling led" make a meeting feel like lead. Somebody said that the difference between early Christians and later ones is that the early ones felt led more often.

"The spirits of the prophets are subject to the prophets"

(1 Cor. 14:32). We can quench the Spirit, or we can "stir up the gift of God," as Paul said to Timothy. The Spirit moves when we move. Holy Spirit meetings are supposed to flow with the supernatural. Every gift is a "ministry."

Activities

This word is the Greek *energemata*, which we all use in the English word *energy*. The Holy Spirit is an energy maker. We read in Scripture, "Your word has given me life" (Ps. 119:50), and that we "shall run and not be weary...shall walk and not faint" (Isa. 40:31). The word is different from the "power" promised in Acts (*dunamis*). That is potential, power in reserve, like a stick of dynamite. It will just lie there, like stone. People pray for "the power" and no doubt receive it, but maybe they should pray for energy, for they simply pray for power without doing anything. The *dunamis* potency is directed to human need.

We can be like spiritual bodybuilders, developing for the sake of being strong. What is the use of a man being able to lift three hundred pounds above his head in the gymnasium if he cannot lift a finger to help his wife in the kitchen? What is the use of all our clamor for power if we do not do the jobs there to be done—the door-to-door evangelism, for example, or Sunday school work—and leave it all to the faithful few?

The release of the power of the Spirit is never possible while we are not active. When we apply ourselves to do the will of God in service, God sees it as us making ourselves an empty vessel for His Spirit. This is the real purpose of our studies together, to see the world church not merely full of power but full of energetic people. The same God who is behind speaking with tongues or healing is behind the activities, the willing service to God.

PART 2

CHAPTER 7

A WORD OF WISDOM

WISDOM AND LOVE are twins upon whose arms all the gifts should lean.

It has been difficult to write this chapter without dealing also with the word of knowledge, as the two are complementary. However, I will endeavor to deal with knowledge separately in the next chapter.

The gift of wisdom is the first in the 1 Corinthians 12 list (v. 8). It is no more than a name and is neither defined nor explained. That is how the rest of the gifts are also introduced. Obviously Paul assumed that the Corinthians would know what he was talking about, as he knew them. He did not know us, however, so for each gift we need to be sure of what he had in mind. In this instance, for example, wisdom has several forms, so what wisdom is the gift?

The golden rule in Bible interpretation is that which Paul himself laid down in this epistle: "That we might know the things that have been freely given to us by God. These things we also speak, not in words which man's wisdom teaches but which the Holy Spirit teaches, comparing spiritual things with spiritual" (1 Cor. 2:12–13). The phrase "spiritual things" here is the same word translated "spiritual gifts" in 1 Corinthians 12:1—*pneumatikos*. Understanding the Bible is not a matter of guesswork. The Bible is its own interpreter.

Wisdom was a real field of interest among Jew and Gentile alike. Each had their tradition of wisdom, which influenced the national outlook. The Greeks sought after wisdom. They were the first nation to experience intellectual awakening. From Thales (a Greek scientist) until the Christian era six hundred years later, the Greeks produced outstanding thinkers who tried to guide their countrymen in life. Their wisdom took many twists and turns, and mind contradicted mind. A little light flickered in the darkness, but the day of full enlightenment never dawned for them, and they continued the search for a convincing worldview. These pagan thinkers are still closely studied today, but philosophy is as far away as ever from bringing a solid ground of hope to us all. Paul went to Athens and preached Jesus, the first voice ever heard there that rang with a trumpet note of certainty and ultimate wisdom.

Jewish wisdom was entirely different from that of men like Socrates and Aristotle, and that we shall come to in due course.

First we must observe exactly what is said in 1 Corinthians 12:8. Several translations, including the King James Version, render the phrase as "the word of wisdom." In Greek it is not "the word" but "a word"; that is, one of many words. It is not the word pointing to a word already in view but a word as yet not known. A car is any car, but the car is the one being used. A word of wisdom is a new shaft of light thrown on a situation.

Solomon has often been quoted as an example of the gift of the word of wisdom, but that is not the same thing. Solomon's gift from God was general wisdom, which God's people can ask for, according to James 1:5.

We are looking here, however, at one of the supernatural gifts, which brings from time to time "a word of wisdom." It does not turn anybody into an oracle, pearls of wisdom falling from his lips every time he opens them. How long "a word of wisdom" may be in words is not stated, but a wise idea or truth could need anything from a sentence to a thesis for its expression. Whatever its form, we are to see it as of the Holy Spirit; that is, supernatural—a manifestation, as this chapter explains. Examples of it abound in Scripture. Jesus, for instance, promised persecuted believers such words of wisdom. He told them not to think beforehand what to say when brought before the courts, for the Father would give them the words at that moment.

WHAT WISDOM?

If there are various schools or species of wisdom, what sort of wisdom is covered by the word of wisdom? Are we just to brush the question aside and say, "Well, any kind"? That would hardly be the way to "rightly [divide] the word of truth" (2 Tim. 2:15). There is little question of the kind of wisdom to which Paul alluded. His mind, at this time, was moving in only one area of wisdom, even while he wrote this epistle. He began with two chapters saying what wisdom is. It is wisdom "in Christ"—"Christ Jesus, who became for us wisdom from God" (1 Cor. 1:30). A word of wisdom would fall within that class of wisdom, related to Christ.

We know a little more of Paul's ideas on the subject. These were molded by Scripture. The Old Testament is full of wisdom. One Hebrew word alone for "wisdom" occurs 146 times. In the New Testament one Greek word appears 51 times, and it does not mean something different in 1 Corinthians than what it means generally in the New Testament.

Wisdom did, in fact, mean something different to the Corinthians, and that is why Paul spent so much of his letter putting their thoughts onto Christian rails. The wisdom that affected the Corinthians was either the abstract philosophy of the Greeks or that of their mystery religions. The age of the great Greek philosophers and of men like the supreme sculptor Phidias was also a crude age of primitive ignorance, barbarity, superstition, and vile devotion to the ancient gods. Generally, Greek wisdom, apart from mathematics, consisted only of statements of thought as definitions.

Jewish wisdom was always practical—how to live. It was

"understanding," something deeper than words that touched the instincts of behavior. The Old Testament reflects this national feature. The Bible even personalizes wisdom (e.g., Prov. 8). The same principle turned their thoughts of God into a practical vein. For the Greeks, God existed entirely as an abstract idea, arrived at by reason and too remote to be reached. For the Jews, God was a living presence among them, and they talked of Him in human terms as having hands, feet, arms, and ears. This, of course, is regarded by liberals as anthropomorphism (making God in the image of humans). Such critics do not appreciate the Jewish outlook. Israel never thought that God had actual physical parts. They used this kind of language because God made man in His own image, and our human limbs and parts are a material picture of His infinitely greater spiritual reality. We have arms, but "You have a mighty arm," they said. The Jewish wisdom was always of an earthy type. The Greeks were centuries behind Israel and spoke of God in impersonal terms, sometimes as no more than abstract good. The Greek god was faceless.

The longest book of wisdom debating God and life in Scripture is the Book of Job. It faces the ultimate questions, but they are brought down to earth and revolve around the experience of Job. The talk is not academic but factual.

The Book of Proverbs is a book of wisdom, but Proverbs also describes wisdom in personal terms in chapters 8 and 9; for example, "I am understanding" (Prov. 8:14). Wisdom is thought of not merely as common sense, experience, good advice, keen insight, or skill, for that is human thinking. It moves into another dimension. God comes into the picture. "The fear of the LORD is the beginning of wisdom" (Prov. 9:10). Lack of wisdom is the opposite thing. "The fool has said in his heart, 'There is no God'" (Ps. 14:1). The wisdom Paul preached was the same personal, practical, down-to-earth understanding. He drew his wisdom from the character of the living God of Israel. Of course, for Paul, the wisdom of God was summed up in the revelation of God's Son Incarnate, Jesus Christ. His "gift of wisdom" relates to that kind of understanding, as we shall see.

The "word of wisdom" is a matter of wisdom for living, not academic insight. However, we should look closely at the Bible's remarkable definition just quoted. "The fear of the LORD is the beginning of wisdom, and the knowledge of the Holy One is understanding" (Prov. 9:10). That is a revolutionary statement that cuts across both ancient and modern thought. No other nation or literature achieved such a radical concept. Wisdom is made to rest on faith in God as the rock of eternal verities. It is not subject to fashion, opinion, speculation, or to any academic school of thought. Amid the disturbing perplexities of life the wisdom of God is the stabilizer.

The man who knows God, in Christ, has found wisdom. He no longer chases the unknown, as the godless do, nor does he seek without purpose and direction. Secular progress has not yet decided what its goal is and therefore cannot know whether it is advancing or not. Christian onlookers see the present progress of the world as a step back into darkness. "The wisdom of their wise men shall perish" (Isa. 29:14). Daniel said wisdom belongs to God, and "He gives wisdom to the wise" (Dan. 2:20–21). For Christians, Jesus is the wisdom of God and "the way, the truth, and the life" (John 14:6).

The wisdom literature—some of it in Bible books such as Job, Psalms, Proverbs, and Ecclesiastes—is a mass of garnered experience for successful living. Ecclesiastes, for instance, handles it in a most original way. On the surface, Ecclesiastes is a cynic's book, saying that the world does not make sense, and it scoffs at everything in creation as vanity, or emptiness, using the word thirty-five times about existence.[1] The same Hebrew word (*hebel*) is used to describe the nothingness of idols. How could such deeply religious people as the Jews include such a book together with the Book of Psalms, which is rich with praises and thanks for God's creation?

The answer is that it balances the matter with another expression used thirty-one times—"under the sun." Ecclesiastes is "under the sun" thinking, limited to the horizons of this material world. The materialist outlook provides no answers, no logic, and leaves mortal existence a riddle. If the world is the whole show, a closed order, a merry-go-round destined to wind down and stop, it is meaningless and should never have existed. We are then like a colony of ants busy in the closed world of a plastic museum showcase.

It's the world's wise try to make the best of a bad job. Paul Tillich, a pantheist, talked of the "courage to be"—be brave while you exist, for you will vanish one day! Life is just a one-shot try. "Human life begins on the far side of despair," said a modern unbeliever. This agrees with the despair of godless philosophers such as Camus, Russell, and Ayer. The "under the sun" attitude is the heart of idolatry, whose god is only what can be seen.

In contrast the believer "endure[s] as seeing Him who is invisible" (Heb. 11:27). Christ Jesus frames everything in wisdom. Ecclesiastes touches the heart of things finally in verse 14 of chapter 12: "God will bring every work into judgment…whether good or evil." In other words, every action is valued by relation to God and His purposes. Brief life has eternal worth. What does not relate to Him is adrift, worth nothing. The world is God's gift to us, from heaven with love, wrought with exquisite consideration for maximum human contentment. It is part of the divine order of wisdom. Our worldly wisdom is only wise if it relates to the wisdom of the Creator. "Remember now your Creator in the days of your youth," said Solomon (Eccles. 12:1). "The LORD by wisdom founded the earth.…The LORD possessed me [wisdom] at the beginning of His way, before His works of old. I have been established from everlasting, from the beginning, before there was ever an earth" (Prov. 3:19; 8:22–23). The world was an act of wisdom.

EDIFICATION WISDOM

This gift relating to the eternal business of God is not optional but indispensable for the building of the church. The church is not a secular and temporary organization, but it is a creation of God, planned from eternity (Rev. 21–22). All that goes on in the church must be related to the purposes of God for redemption, and every gift will operate toward the same goal. Christ established the present Christian age to be dominated by the Holy Spirit in world evangelism. The gift of the word of wisdom is God at the wheel keeping us heading in the right direction even when we are busy in matters that seem remote.

Paul said that the Corinthian believers "[came] short in no gift" (1 Cor. 1:7). Nevertheless, they displayed a memorable aptitude for doing the wrong thing—even with the gifts. Their vocal displays of tongues, for example, were outside the framework of God's redemptive plan. They had nothing to do with edifying—building up—the church. Gifts were treated as toys instead of the power tools given to laborers by the Holy Spirit. We are offered more than emotional satisfaction. We are wise master builders working according to the grace of God, which is given unto us (1 Cor. 3:10).

"Wise master builder" is in Greek *sophos architekton*. *Architekton* is the word from which we get the English *architect*, *technology,* and so on, but it actually means a head builder. A *tekton* is a craftsman in wood, metal, or stone. Jesus was a tekton (Mark 6:3), like Joseph (Matt. 13:55). God is called a "builder and maker"—*teknites.* We get our word technical from the Greek *techne,* an art or craft, but our English word *craftiness* is different, and the Greeks had a totally different word for it—*panourgia,* which stands for human wisdom, the opposite of the divine wisdom spoken of in 1 Corinthians 3:19.

A *teknites* (craftsman builder) of the church needs *sophia* (wisdom). When the Lord ordered the making of the tabernacle in the wilderness, He said, "See, I have called Bezalel...and have filled him with the Spirit of God, in wisdom...to work in all manner of workmanship" (Exod. 31:2–5). It was all "cunning" or intricate filigree, gold lace work. The direction all God's works take is toward the beautiful, and that applies to the church—any church—just as the tabernacle was enriched with golden furniture and brilliant tapestries. The robes of the high priest were "glory and beauty." The church is the tabernacle of God (Rev. 21:3) to be adorned with wisdom, part of the bridal beauty of Christ's bride.

What we have just said is from the same Scriptures that Paul knew so well and that he expounds in 1 Corinthians 1 and 2. This "fear of God" wisdom given by God is what was in his mind when he spoke of "the word of wisdom." It is not just a piece of good advice. It is a special word in season. The word of wisdom operates to bring us into proper relationship with God's eternal purposes. It overlaps with prophecy. Its center and pivot is "the fear of the Lord," and it is, therefore, more than a wise consideration of all the facts and circumstances. It takes in all the facts we know, and those that relate to God and, no doubt, facts to which the Lord alone has access, and places in our minds a principle or feel for what should be done.

Such a divine word comes to us for our everyday practical circumstances, either personal or for the church. It throws light upon situations and enables us to make right choices toward the unseen goals of God. "I understand more than the ancients, because I keep Your precepts," said the young man, possibly a student scribe, who wrote Psalm 119:100.

WISDOM'S SECRET HEART

However, here is a mystery revelation. Christ is the final meaning of wisdom. In Him are "hidden all the treasures of wisdom and knowledge" (Col. 2:3). In 1 Corinthians 1:23–24 Christ is described as the wisdom of God, particularly "Christ crucified." If a word of wisdom is genuine, it has a Calvary background, for Christ "is made unto us wisdom" (1 Cor. 1:30, KJV; see also Eph. 1:8, 17). When we are pushed and pulled this way and that by stress, tempted perhaps by material or personal advantage, a word of wisdom will have the Calvary background with its reminder of other values.

James 3:15–17 declares that there is a wisdom that is "earthly, sensual, demonic" instead of that from above which is "pure, then peaceable, gentle, willing to yield, full of mercy and good fruits, without partiality and without hypocrisy." It was worldly wisdom that crucified Christ. A true word of wisdom enables us to take up the cross and discover the eternal dimensions of living by faith in God. That does not mean we shall be given a precise plan, but we shall be given the principle of action.

WISDOM, NOT
BIT AND BRIDLE

A word of wisdom will be practical. This is not a "gift" of wisdom but a word of wisdom. General wisdom is a quality available to us all, as James 1:5 says. The Lord has no intention of telling us when to sharpen our pencil or what to have for tea. Jesus never used a bit and bridle to steer His disciples at every turn in the road. Freedom in Christ delivers His followers from a life under law, and God leaves large areas of our lives to our own choice and decision. Whatever we find to do in His name, He will bless.

Nevertheless there are accounts in Scripture of directives coming from God. A word of wisdom may lead us to do something that normally would not occur to us. Samuel told Saul what he should do when looking for his father's donkeys. Throughout the Book of Acts are instances of a word of wisdom. Paul warned the captain of a ship not to let the crew abandon the vessel. Ananias was sent to pray for Saul and his healing and to give him insight into his future. James was

given a wise word, as the chairman of the important conference in Jerusalem, when the relationship of Gentiles with the
Jewish institutions was proving a difficult question. Paul had
a word of wisdom directive to stay in Corinth, because God
had many people there.

I have heard very earnest preachers bringing people to
make a vow at the altar to wait for God to speak each day.
Many say, "I am waiting for a word of wisdom from the
Lord." What they really want is for God to make up their
minds for them and relieve them of responsibilities. God
does speak, and He spoke to men of old, but on no occasion did He speak when or because somebody was waiting or
asking Him to speak. God does not talk to order. The men
and women God spoke to in Bible days were people getting
on with whatever they had to do. Whoever tells us to do
anything, we are personally responsible. Those who act only
when they hear directions from God are living under law
and not "the perfect law of liberty" (James 1:25). God wants
us to grow up in Him, to be adults, not puppets moved by
strings from heaven.

Believers are so often stressed and anxious, looking over
their shoulders, wondering if they have done God's will, as
if God quietly hid a blueprint every morning, which it was
their first duty to find. This puts believers under a heavier
burden than even the scribes imposed, for at least they could
pinpoint a scripture for what they thought God ordered. A

wisdom greater than ours comes to us as free agents, not as a law of Sinai.

HOW THE
GIFT OPERATES

A word of wisdom is not necessarily a dramatic pronouncement by someone standing on his or her feet in a church and making a declaration. It may come in other ways. Maybe it will be in discussion. Having wisdom from above, we consult with one another and discuss; then a key is given to unlock the situation. It could come from anybody, even the least effective person present.

A word of wisdom may come by the Scriptures, the book of all wisdom. There is no doubt that Scripture is the most common means used by the Holy Spirit. Understanding frequently comes from hearing the Word to direct our footsteps. That is one reason why the ministry of the Word is so vital to us all. The Bible has the peculiar habit of addressing us, even in the most unexpected phrase, in everyday situations.

Ministry, which is experience related, or which offers specialist skills, needs to be Word related. Hundreds of seminars everywhere give the benefit of business and other secular expertise for the work of God. Good as they may be, without the Word they will be wanting. The wisdom of the business world should not make redundant the wisdom of the Word and the word of wisdom, or being led of God. A word of wisdom is beyond human experience. It is revelation.

Wisdom may come through a chance remark or a throw-away comment. To the person speaking it may seem nothing, but it is sped by the Spirit like an arrow straight to the heart of a problem or need. It will, like all gifts, be for the profit of all, enabling us to "walk in wisdom," especially "toward those who are outside" (Col. 4:5).

Wisdom is described as treasure (Matt. 13:52; Rom. 11:33; Col. 2:3). The gift or manifestation is that treasure. It has a practical purpose. It may come in a manner that does not seem miraculous at all. God makes little fuss about any-thing—He works very quietly, almost secretly, and never tries to amaze us for the sake of it. It does not need to come in spectacular form. It is not only a wonder, but it also touches the heart of the problem.

A word of wisdom may come to us for ourselves, for some-body else, or for a whole Christian group. For Paul it came personally, and for Saul it came through Samuel.

A word of caution about seeking a word of wisdom. One of the major purposes of this gift is to direct us. Some ask God to counsel them, to show them in what way they should go, but how do they know that He wishes them to go at all? It is dangerous to ask God to show you a new direc-tion unless He has first given a word of wisdom indicating that He has a new direction for you. Perhaps there is no new direction. He simply wants you to carry on as you are. Then again, if He wants you to change direction, He would tell you anyway and not conceal it until you are in a mood to fast and pray to find out what it is. If He does not speak, it is because He has nothing to say and is satisfied with what you are doing. God is not a radio to be turned on at will. The Lord will let you know quickly enough if you are running in the wrong direction.

CHAPTER 8

A WORD
OF KNOWLEDGE

L ET ME BEGIN with a saying from one of the wisdom books: "Ants are exceedingly wise." (See Proverbs 30:24–25.) The trouble is, ants have wisdom without knowledge. They are hardly walking encyclopedias. Humans, in contrast, are vastly provided with knowledge, but moral wisdom also seems to have little place in the modern world. This is tragic considering that we have been printing the Bible for hundreds of years.

If God gives a word of knowledge, it is unlikely to have trivial meaning or purpose. It will not be on the level of a crystal ball forecast—that you will meet a tall dark stranger. In the Bible, knowledge itself is not mere education but something of more consequence.

Right at the start we read, "Of the tree of the knowledge of good and evil you shall not eat" (Gen. 2:17). Well, we know Adam and Eve did eat, and the first sin brought knowledge, but it was the knowledge of evil. It was not scientific knowledge either, but experience. They knew pain, fear, guilt, shame. They also knew goodness, but only as a contrast to their wretched condition.

This is how it seems to go on. True science, beginning in the seventeenth century with Newton, Kepler, and company, seemed like a shining dawn, but its horrific developments have brought the bloodred clouds of war and anguish. Knowledge fills our heads but not our hearts. A wiser race would have pursued some different course of knowledge.

However, we are concerned with divine not temporal knowledge. To be wise we have to know, and so the gift of a word of knowledge complements the gift of a word of wisdom. If a special word brings to light a particular circumstance, a word of wisdom may well be needed also to do what should be done.

Whatever we find is meant by a word of knowledge, we cannot leave out of our study the fact that Scripture so often talks of it, and usually in a special sense. We know, in any case, that the Word of God remains the divine source of spiritual wisdom and knowledge. "Oh, the depth of the riches both of the wisdom and knowledge of God!" (Rom. 11:33). The written Word of God reveals the Living Word, "in whom are hidden all the treasures of wisdom and knowledge" (Col. 2:3).

The manifestation gifts are too valuable to neglect: "Cry

out for discernment, and lift up your voice for under-standing...seek her as silver, and search for her as for hidden treasures....For wisdom is better than rubies" (Prov. 2:3; 8:11). Jesus describes knowledge as "treasure" (Matt. 13:52). The alternative is this: "My people are destroyed for lack of knowledge"; they "withered away because [they] lacked mois-ture" (Hosea 4:6; Luke 8:6).

The gifts are builders' tools for the edifying of the church. God gives them because we need them.

There is one thing we must point out once again. In the New Testament the spiritual gifts are never anything else but for each local gathering of believers. There may be excep-tional gifts, which bring men from across the seas with an international ministry for exceptional circumstances, but the local church is meant to benefit from its own local gifts. This can be idealistic, depending on the size and state of the church, but nevertheless that is God's order of things.

WHAT KNOWLEDGE?

The proper approach to understanding what is meant by a word of knowledge is to ask: What is this knowledge about? What does Paul mean by knowledge? He does not specify, because he says so much about knowledge elsewhere. It is a favorite subject of his, but it is always the kind of knowl-edge that is extolled throughout Scripture; that is, not just academic Bible knowledge but also understanding. Psalm 119:100 speaks of knowing more than our teachers—that is, having a deeper feel for truth. Unbelievers have no "knowing," because certain things come to us through the media of faith and love. To unbelievers it is as foolish and incommunicable as microchip technology would have been to Queen Victoria. "The word which they heard did not profit them, not being mixed with faith in those who had heard it" (Heb. 4:2). Mental application will never make up for the absence of faith.

> In that hour Jesus rejoiced in the Spirit and said, "I thank You, Father, Lord of heaven and earth, that You have hidden these things from the wise and prudent and revealed them to babes. Even so, Father, for so it seemed good in Your sight. All things have been delivered to Me by My Father, and no one knows who the Son is except the Father, and who the Father is except the Son, and the one whom the Son wills to reveal Him."
>
> —LUKE 10:21–22

In pursuit of our goal, here is a useful fact: the Gospel of John never uses the word *knowledge* but always *knowing*. To John, true knowledge was not something memorized; it was something going on, something dynamic. The participle "knowing" is not a static noun; it goes with living, loving, seeing, believing. That puts us on the right track— true knowledge is "going on knowing," like knowing a family member. A word of knowledge will relate to that.

KNOWLEDGE AND POWER

We pick up another clue from Matthew 22:29: "You are mistaken, not knowing the Scriptures nor the power of God." This would have staggered the rabbis. The scribes and others worked constantly on the Torah (the Law, or Scripture). They knew much of it by heart and thereby expected to earn eternal life. What Jesus said about them was what they said about the common people, whom they considered cursed for not knowing the Law. He showed them the secret principle of knowledge: "If anyone wants to do His will, he shall know concerning the doctrine" (John 7:17). Today many church leaders deny both the Scriptures and the power of God, something that even the Pharisees did not do. They treat the supernatural gifts as natural talents, tongues as linguistic ability, knowledge as education, and wisdom as psychology. Those who study a miracle book without belief in miracles are foredoomed to failure.

THE LAMP THAT NEVER FLICKERS

The gift of "a word of knowledge" has a comprehensive sweep. It is what the Old Testament describes as understanding, insight of the heart. A computer has knowledge but no understanding. "'Let not the wise man glory in his wisdom...but let him who glories glory in this: that he understands and knows Me...' says the LORD" (Jer. 9:23–24).

To Israel, God seemed to keep Himself at arm's length as

the high and lofty One who inhabits eternity, known only through a third party, a prophet, or priest. They only had information about God. In Jesus, God drew near in a manger, accessible, belonging to a family. The Son of God became the Son of Man. Then the knowledge of God became personal. Worship was no longer singing psalms to a transcendent deity on a celestial throne, but it was given a new dynamic. He is one of us, our crucified and beloved Lord and Savior Jesus Christ. Christ- and Cross-centered Christian worship began. "The Lord of hosts" became "Abba, Father," the only name Jesus ever used about God. Here is knowledge, to know Him "whom to know is life eternal."[1]

Opening up our understanding of knowledge still further, we turn to Matthew 11:25–27. First note that His Father was the "Lord of heaven and earth" but had revealed things to "babes." In Luke 10:23 Jesus also said, "Blessed are the eyes which see the things you see." Note again Christ's description of the Father—"Lord of heaven and earth" (v. 21). He knew all that went on and could reveal it to whom He pleased.

There is special knowledge—the ultimate knowledge. "No one knows who the Son is except the Father, and who the Father is except the Son, and the one to whom the Son wills to reveal Him" (v. 22). Jesus thanked the Father that certain things were "hidden from the wise and the prudent and...revealed...to babes" (Matt. 11:25).

The supreme knowledge is the knowledge of God. To know Him, however, is not all knowledge, which Paul says would enable us to understand all mysteries (1 Cor. 13:2). There is God's knowledge, as the Lord of heaven and earth, and it includes "the secrets of his heart," which 1 Corinthians 14:25 (kjv) says can be revealed through the prophetic gifts.

Now, let us put all these clues together and see if we can define what knowledge is in "a word of knowledge." These clues indicate quite a comprehensive knowledge.

1. The basic knowledge, which is to know God, is only by revelation through His Son our Lord Jesus Christ. The Bible calls it "understanding," which means a living acquaintance with God.

2. There is a deeper heart grasp of His Word.

3. We have a divinely inspired sense of what is right and wrong, or wise and foolish in life.

4. The Father knows all things, and they that know Him may have His confidence and share a little of what He sees.

This clarifies what we may expect from a word of knowledge. It is for us in order to help us plot a wise course through life. The Lord of heaven and earth "works all things according to the counsel of His will" (Eph. 1:11). To know Him with whom we have to do is to walk sure-footed in accordance with the direction of God's plans. We are all involved in His providences. We are thankful for the Word, which is a lamp to our path, but at many a juncture we need a personal word of knowledge from God. It will come as a truth, a principle, or as illuminating counsel through the highlighting of a passage of Scripture, by the spoken word of knowledge, or a combination of both.

The candle flame of human genius flickers briefly before being extinguished by the winds of time. The lamp of God never flickers. Jeremiah said, "O LORD, I know the way of man is not in himself; it is not in man who walks to direct his own steps" (Jer. 10:23). "It is God who…makes my way perfect" (Ps. 18:32). God possessed intimate knowledge of our lives even before we were born. "How precious also are Your thoughts to me, O God!…Such knowledge is too wonderful for me; it is high, I cannot attain it" (Ps. 139:17, 6). By the Word and a word of knowledge we can harmonize our ways with His eternal counsels.

Without instruction the structure of our lives would collapse in chaos. This is exactly the state of those who have no knowledge of the Lord. Life for the unregenerate is a meaningless disorder. As Sir W. S. Gilbert said, "Try we life-long, we can never / Straighten out life's tangled skein."[2]

KNOWLEDGE AND THE CHURCH

We have seen that knowledge involves the ways and purposes of God. One of His great activities is the church. That is certainly an area in which our lives must harmonize. In fact, the mystery of the church is the greatest divine project that God has made known to us. The church is what the gift chapters of 1 Corinthians, and indeed the whole epistle, are about. The gifts are for building up the church. As we keep saying, if God gives them, we need them. They are not optional extras.

The gift of a word of knowledge is seen in Bible incidents, such as the careers of Joseph, Moses, Elisha, Daniel, Peter, and others. Jesus had perfect knowledge about the woman of Samaria and about Nathanael of Cana. Elisha knew the king of Syria's secret battle strategies—obvious instances of God-given communication. "The secret of the LORD is with those who fear him" (Ps. 25:14). "Surely the Lord GOD does nothing unless He reveals His secret to His servants the prophets" (Amos 3:7).

One afternoon in a hotel room I was praying, and the Holy Spirit began to speak to me. He put in my mind that that night a young man would come to the service whose name was John. The Lord gave me a message for him. I said to the Lord that half the men in that city were called John, and if I just called his name, it would sound ridiculous. The Lord replied "But his name is John!" "Very well," I said. "I will obey You."

What I did not know, however, was that very morning a mother was praying for her son, and the Holy Spirit told her, "Ask John your son to come with you to the service, because the Holy Spirit will call him out by name." Her boy was eighteen years old. She then begged him to come, and, full of disbelief, he declared "All right, Mum, I'll come. If God calls me out by name, my life will belong to Him."

In the evening service I gave the word that the Holy Spirit had given me and called out for John. Not surprisingly, John was awed. This was a manifestation of the Spirit and the word of knowledge. John gave his life to Jesus that day. This account is true, and I still have the mother's letter on file.

However, we have spent the first part of this chapter showing that this gift is much more than these prophetic flashes of knowledge about what is happening. The gift comes to people among people, not as a dark saying in secret. Having the knowledge of God is not for personal gratification or even egotism, but it is for "the profit of all" (1 Cor. 12:7).

We can now make two statements:

- The Lord does not operate outside the Word. No revelation springs forth that runs counter to the Word. Spurgeon said that there is no new truth, for if it is new, it is not in the Word and therefore not true. Even a word of knowledge or wisdom for a person or individual will, directly or indirectly, relate to Scripture.

- A word of knowledge always aims at fellowship with God, even when it concerns the mundane. God may put in our minds what is in His mind about the world, and He seeks cooperation.

GIFTS IN PRACTICE

We often hear someone say, "I have a word from the Lord." That may indeed be so, but it does open up questions. First, what are these new utterances called "words from the Lord"? Are they words of wisdom, of knowledge, of prophecy, or what? Into which New Testament category do they fit?

Are they simply spiritual thoughts, which arise in all our minds if we follow the Lord? There is no harm in someone rising in church to pass on something that he has received or to interpret some picture that happens to float across his mind. If convenient, an opportunity might be given to approved members to minister in this way. However, to dignify them with the authority of divine origin, if they are little more than a passing thought, is quite another thing. If we say we have a word from the Lord, it had better be. If prophecy is to be judged, how much more a mere "word from the Lord"? Admittedly, many utterances do not need to be proved, since they would mislead nobody. They are too slight, even though they may be given a majestic sound by phrases such as "I, the Lord, do say unto thee."

With all that we have learned so far about the gifts, we have to keep in mind that no prophetic utterance takes priority over the ministry of the Word of God itself. Prophecy must not displace preaching. People cannot live by inspirationalism but only by the bread of God, the Word.

If anyone disagrees and wants a church to become mainly

prophetic, let him explain why, in addition to these gifts and manifestations, God has also given to the church apostles, evangelists, pastors, and teachers "for the equipping of the saints for the work of the ministry, for the edifying of the body of Christ" (Eph. 4:12). Prophets do not usurp the place of apostles, evangelists, pastors, and teachers. The gifts of the Spirit are complementary to the Word.

Finally, there are two questions. First, how does a person know he or she has "a word of knowledge"? We shall look more closely at the mechanics of the prophetic gifts later, but we can note here that the promptings of God may be experienced in our spirit, our mind, or our body. Sometimes we may have no "experience" as such—that is, we may speak a word of knowledge or of wisdom without realizing it, just as Caiaphas was said to prophesy without knowing it (John 11:49–51). God may use a throwaway remark to somebody who needs it. During a conversation one pastor laughed and said to another, "We know ever so many ways to do without the Holy Spirit." It affected the whole outlook of his friend.

Secondly, can this gift be taught? Nobody can learn a gift. However, instruction can be useful. Teaching about the gifts is necessary to recover a proper place for them in the church and to encourage reticent people who have held back the gift that God has given them—in particular speech gifts. Some need to value their gift and understand how it operates. It is not impossible for those being "taught a gift" to receive the real thing; that only happens by the Spirit. The Holy

Spirit responds to seeking and willing souls. Otherwise, any learned technique remains what it is, a work of the flesh, not a manifestation of God's Spirit. Nobody can teach a manifestation, though we may all learn about it.

THE PROPHETIC MINISTRY

Finally, we turn to some modern expressions and ask about their validity—phrases such as "the prophetic church" and the "prophetic ministry." They are not unscriptural, and every ministry should be prophetic, but we might wonder if it would be more biblical if we spoke of "the Word of God church" or "the Word ministry." That is always the conception of the church in the New Testament—"the pillar and ground of the truth." In Acts, the expansion of the church is described as "the Word of God grew and multiplied." We have said that prophecy should not usurp teaching. When a church floats on prophesyings, then it needs to be anchored to the rock of the Word of God. "Preach the Word!"

We alluded briefly above to a word of wisdom or knowledge coming via the exposition of the Word of God. The knowledge, which Jesus Himself so highly valued and described as "treasure new and old," is brought forth by the teacher or preacher of the Word (Matt. 13:52). It may not even seem supernatural, but the Word always is; yet that does not mean sensational. God often brings the critical word of knowledge to bear on our situation through what seems ordinary ministry.

The Word of God is active. The voice of the Spirit is often missed because the pulpit voice is listened to critically instead of with an open heart. To whom is God more likely to give a word of knowledge than to the man waiting upon the ministry in the Word?

KNOWLEDGE AND PUBLIC MINISTRY

Some men and women are announced as having "a prophetic ministry"; that is, they specialize in prophetic gifts, especially a word of knowledge.

The following comments relate also to the whole question of the prophet and prophesying.

The word-of-knowledge type of career is something of an innovation, though being new does not mean that it is to be rejected. The basic question is how prophets should operate, which comes down to a question of wisdom. It is simply a matter of method. For the rest of us, we must judge, hold fast to what is good, and leave anything else alone.

Usually, word-of-knowledge prophets bring a public emphasis to their work. The most frequent practice is to call individuals forward in front of a congregation in order to prophesy over them. There are no actual instances in the New Testament of this being done, either occasionally or as the regular feature of anyone's ministry, but other accepted church practices are also not found in the New Testament. The only criteria are the common matters of respect and wisdom.

There are assumptions we can perhaps ask about. Should a prophetic ministry be announced or advertised? Must the Holy Spirit oblige every time? Can He be guaranteed to do what is expected of Him as advertised? The answer is, as we have seen, that there is no outright gift, but there are manifestations according to the will of God. No gift is an outright independent ability operating solely at will—like playing the piano—which could be announced beforehand.

There is a question many have asked. Should we expose individuals in a congregation to personal scrutiny, either with or without the Spirit, unless by the direct leading of God? Where there is a public mischief being perpetrated, a sin affecting the congregation, a sin of Achan, so to speak, then God may wish it to be exposed.

However, if we are trusted with the secrets of human lives, is it for public knowledge? If God trusts us with a secret, should it not be for personal counsel to that individual alone? To acquaint a whole congregation that somebody's Christian marriage is breaking up or that a person has this or that weakness, or even that they are good in some way, brings nobody any benefit. It might give material for gossips or even leave someone standing in bad grace.

If ever a revelation describes a person's fault, then the Scriptures tell us what to do. "If a man is overtaken in any trespass, you who are spiritual restore such a one in a spirit of gentleness, considering yourself lest you also be tempted" (Gal. 6:1). We are not to tell the whole church—nothing could be better guaranteed to do the devil's work as the accuser of the brethren and so split a church. Christian procedures are strictly laid down, both by Christ and by apostolic command. Love covers a multitude of sins. The real purpose of such a personal revelation would be what 1 John 5:16 says, to pray about their sin, or as Galatians 6:2 exhorts us, to "bear one another's burdens."

Another question arises: Does the expression a "prophetic ministry" only belong to those who operate in a session of words of knowledge? Is not the ministry of the Word also a "prophetic ministry," seeing that the Word itself is always prophetic? Great prophets have sometimes been great preachers.

If we know anything about human nature, a man expected to operate prophetically will feel under pressure not to fail, although in fact he can only do what the Spirit allows him to do. Balaam was one instance in Scripture of a prophet expected to operate according to plan. (There were others.) He found himself in serious difficulties.

The possibility is, that in trying to come up to congregational expectations, a person may bring revelations that originate from the imagination rather than the Spirit. We wish it were never so, but many have been disenchanted after exciting statements "from the Lord"—some on very prominent and noted occasions. But let this not detract from the fact that God's servants do have revelations by the Spirit.

I do not want to pronounce judgment but to put forth thoughts that perhaps need time and study to settle.

Unfortunately, words of knowledge have been heard that are so personal and related to so little in the church, the Word, or even the work of God, that it has all become dubbed, with some justification, as "charismatic fortune-telling." Yet rightly operated it could be invaluable.

Again, as to failed prophecies and failed words of knowledge, human fallibility will occur. That does not invalidate a ministry, unless it becomes frequent. Only the Word of God is inerrant. Even Agabus, named in Scripture as a Christian prophet, was not completely accurate in his utterances. He said the Jews would bind Paul at Jerusalem and hand him over to the Gentiles (Acts 21:10–11). They did neither of those things. Other prophets in Acts were likewise limited. To be mistaken is possible, but wild and total inaccuracies and great pronouncements made halfway across the world that have proved nonsense have brought the gift into disrepute as mere verbosity, and they bring into question whether the people concerned are prophets or not.

We learned a few pages back that wisdom and knowledge are complementary. A word of knowledge needs, sometimes at least, to be complemented by a word of wisdom. It can be salutary when a church's spiritual condition is described in the Spirit, but those exercising that type of ministry should consider how Christ judged the seven churches of Asia in Revelation. He always included a positive note of spiritual counsel and wisdom.

KNOWLEDGE AND THE THIRD PARTY

Scripture has much to say about all prophetic matters, and here is another current issue—prophetic knowledge and a third party. In the Old Testament covenant order, a priest or prophet was the channel by which the will of God was known. The mind of the Lord was made known through Urim and Thummim or brought to the ordinary people by the elite and anointed class. This covenant has passed away. The glory of the new covenant is that everyone is a priest, everyone is anointed, and everyone has access to God for himself or herself to know His mind and will.

It may be that confirmation may come through a word of knowledge, but it is no more than that. Guidance is direct. God told Cornelius to send for Peter, but He told Peter also, or Peter would have had nothing to do with it. "The secret of the LORD is with those who fear Him" (Ps. 25:14).

No third party, no prophet or priest, no pastor or even apostle need stand between God and believers. Nobody has the right to lord it over believers in the name of the Lord, as if they had a private communication from God about other people. Certainly others may be shown what God's will is for us, as was shown to the men in Antioch about Paul and Silas, but it is never without the Lord showing us also, as He had shown Paul and Silas (Acts 13:1–2). What each of us does is our own choice. Responsibility does not rest on other shoulders. Paul, for example, always kept his own counsel with

God, whatever others said, instanced especially before he was arrested. Others told him not only what would happen, which was more or less correct, but also what he should do, which was their interpretation of their own prophecy and incorrect. God gives us wisdom, not instruction for action. To do what we feel is right before God is our glorious privilege and standing in Christ, of which no man must subtly rob us. We must discern—the gift of discernment is often needed in the operation of other gifts.

We shall look further into the prophetic gifts when we come to look at prophecy.

CHAPTER 9

FAITH

FAITH RISKS EVERYTHING on God, but God never lets us down. I remember an occasion when we were putting up one of our big tents. The ground was soft, and if a heavy rainstorm came, every fastening would pull out. Then I saw a rainstorm on the way. To me it contained the leering face of the devil, and I stood and rebuked him and the black clouds that were moving toward us. If the tent collapsed, it would be dangerous for the vast crowd inside it, but I said to the men, "Go ahead; I shall preach in it tonight." I spoke with assurance in my heart, the faith of God. I said aloud to the devil, "If you destroy this tent, I shall get a bigger one." (I got a bigger one in any case!) I raised my voice and ordered that storm to leave us alone, and then I watched it divide, passing north and south of our tent area. The ground remained dry and safe.

Faith is the pivot of our relationship with God. The whole

Bible illustrates this. Nevertheless, there is no subject that calls for explanation from the Scriptures more than faith and the gift of faith. We particularly want to bring help on this matter.

What Jesus said is perhaps the first thing people quote, that with enough faith we could move a mountain (Matt. 17:20; 21:21). However, nobody has ever done it. No doubt many have experimented—usually with no brilliant hope of success and perhaps with no idea where to move a mountain to.

No apostle did it, nor did Jesus Himself. God planned the landscape at Creation, and I do not think that He would want us shuffling the scenery about. The most frequent illustrations of faith in the New Testament are healings, but that need not be taken as the major use of the gift of faith. Why then did Jesus talk of moving mountains by faith?

For those who want to understand the Bible, here is something very important. Always read a whole passage, never just one verse. Do not pull texts out of the context of Scripture, like this one about moving mountains. Matthew 17:20 concerns prayer against demons, and Matthew 21:21 relates to opposition and enemies. Mountain moving has to be understood in these connections.

Now, about doing the impossible—awful mistakes have been made. To get to the heart of the matter, we will enter the Garden of Gethsemane with humble awe. The Son of God is praying about what is possible, and what He says penetrates to the very heart of the matter. Jesus said "O My Father, if it is possible, let this cup pass from Me; nevertheless, not as

I will, but as You will" (Matt. 26:39). We understand from this that only what is God's will is possible. A disciple who heard Jesus in the Garden later wrote, "If we ask anything according to His will, He hears us" (1 John 5:14). Christ's prayer shows that what is possible is limited by the very evils Jesus came to overcome. It was not possible, for example, for God to save us from evil and also save His Son. Similarly, our fight against evil often presents us with such a situation. To be what God sends us to be, His children witnessing in an alien world, means that we are faced by evils.

Recently some of our evangelism campaigns have been canceled. We were going to confront evils, but those evils were what brought about the withdrawal of visas and permits. God's will was not done. That is why we must pray, "Thy will be done on earth, as it is in heaven." Our lives have been under serious threat, but that danger could only be removed when the gospel entered the lives of our opponents. What can be done in such circumstances? It creates a dilemma, and we have to let God solve it. It is part of the process, or fight, against the devil. I said elsewhere that suffering and the ministry of healing seem inseparable. Nevertheless, mountains will be removed as we go on working and believing.

FROM FAITH TO FAITH

At least four forms of faith are mentioned in Scripture:

> God has dealt to each one a measure of faith.
> —Romans 12:3

By grace you have been saved through faith...the gift
of God.

—EPHESIANS 2:8

The fruit of the Spirit is...faithfulness.

—GALATIANS 5:22

The apostle said to the Lord, "Increase our faith."

—LUKE 17:5

To another [is given] faith by the same Spirit.

—1 CORINTHIANS 12:9

We can describe these four kinds of faith as follows:

- Common faith, which all men have

- Saving faith

- Faith, the fruit of the Spirit (ever-increasing
  faith)

- The gift of faith

This may oversimplify matters for the scholarly, but our
analysis will help us to grasp what we mean by the gift of
faith.

THE PARADOX

Many books are on the market to exemplify and build up
faith. Nevertheless the greatest is the Bible—the book of
faith. It is the handbook showing us how faith operates, and

it also gives us the faith we need to operate. "Faith comes by hearing, and hearing by the word of God" (Rom. 10:17).

Now comes the paradox. We also read, "The word which they heard did not profit them, not being mixed with faith in those who heard it" (Heb. 4:2). We need faith to read the Word, but we need the Word to get faith. However, that little problem is not insoluble. Faith flows into the hearts of any who are open to it. Let the cynic remain a cynic, but the spiritual law is that faith brings faith, as Romans 1:17 says, "…from faith to faith."

This is the principle that Jesus explained: "Whoever has, to him more will be given, and he will have abundance; but whoever does not have, even what he has will be taken away from him" (Matt. 13:12). The spirit of unbelief sours the soil and kills the seed of the Word.

We can take that a step further. Although faith is a gift, we are responsible if we do not possess it. It rests with us to believe or not believe. It is our choice. Unbelief is not intellectual but emotional; it's a matter of attitude of the heart. Nothing can possibly disprove God or show that to trust Him is wrong, but "not all have faith"; that is, they have willed themselves not to believe and are "unreasonable and wicked" (2 Thess. 3:2), because they can believe, for God has "dealt to each one a measure of faith" (Rom. 12:3). It is a test of character, not of reasoning ability. Unbelief is sin, which is why "he who does not believe is condemned already" (John 3:18). Faith saves sinners, although the nature of sinners is to rebel against faith. "Have faith!" Jesus commanded, and He commends those who do.

Faith is from God, His gift to us at birth, like sight or hearing. It is a faculty or a hand by which we reach out and take what God has for us. If we destroy the faculty or let that hand wither, then we can take nothing. We are guilty losers. The world conditions us. We go out in the morning, work all day, come in at night, read the newspaper, and watch television—and in all that time how much have we been exposed to what will encourage faith in God? Usually nothing whatsoever—not a single word. On the contrary, we have been almost immersed in a sea of doubt and sin. The world is a vast brainwashing establishment to destroy faith in God. It maims us spiritually; it amputates our hand of faith. We are "civilized" out of the simple nature God gave us.

A word of warning here: Faith is not a subject, like gardening or photography, just for those interested. We either believe or perish. Faith is a universal human obligation and responsibility. This is set out in the parable of the wedding feast in Matthew 22:12. All guests were provided with a wedding garment, meaning faith. One man came, apparently thinking that he could dress better than anybody else, wearing his own, possibly self-made, clothes. He was thrown out.

The standard dress in the kingdom of God is faith. "Without faith it is impossible to please Him [God]" (Heb. 11:6). This one individual had come to the feast proud and superior, not wearing the garments of God-given faith. The kingdom of God is not a meritocracy. Entry permits, visas, and passports are issued to the believing alone. Academic qualifications are irrelevant. Heaven will not be monopolized by theological graduates or by people who have "never robbed a bank," but only by people displaying the simple badge of faith.

INCREASING FAITH

Whatever form of faith we have—natural faith, saving faith, faith as a fruit, or the gift of faith—its childlike quality remains. Believing is not clever. Faith moves the mountains that doubt creates. It is not the product of brilliance of thought, but of "looking unto Jesus, the author and finisher of our faith" (Heb. 12:2). We receive "the faith of our Lord Jesus Christ," as James 2:1 says.

What is faith? It cannot be quantified. There is no half-faith, 90 percent faith, or anything like that. The poet Wordsworth described it as a "passionate intuition," "persuasion and belief had ripened into faith."[1] That is what Jesus meant when He said, "If you have faith as a mustard seed" (Matt. 17:20), it could move mountains. Nevertheless, we read about the "proportion" of faith (Rom. 12:6)—that is, proportionate to the demand made upon it. Jesus talked about little faith and great faith and asked, "How is it you have no faith?" (Mark 4:40). Having no faith was the only thing that ever surprised Jesus (Matt. 8:10; Mark 4:40). The vital thing to realize is that we can increase in faith. One form of that increase comes with the gift of faith.

All increase of faith, such as the disciples asked for in Luke 17:5, is given by the Holy Spirit through the Word of God. It is impossible for faith to grow by prayer or worship alone. We may pray for faith, but we must also take the proper steps for our prayer to be answered, namely by hearing or reading the Word. The less our understanding of the Word, the less our faith. We can have so little of the Word under our feet that we do not stand on faith but only balance on one toe. We may as well try to grow an apple tree on a damp cloth as cultivate faith by a paperback book telling of somebody else's experience.

The teaching of the Word is the only true way. This way a church can be strong and its members can avoid doubts and not fall under the displeasure of the Lord. It is impossible to please God without faith. It is the only likely means by which there can be any genuine manifestation of the Spirit. Hearing about people's wonderful answers to prayer, healings, or experiences is necessary and good, for God commands us to tell and testify, but often our doubts tell us that other people's miracles were only for them and not for us. They do not really create the kind of faith Christ wants. We see that in John 2:23–24, where faith based on miracles is not the best faith. It is only faith in miracles, not faith in God. When miracles do not happen, faith can evaporate.

The Gospels more than once record Jesus calling people

by the name of "little faiths" (Greek: *oligopistos*) (Matt. 6:30). We are what our faith is. It sums us up and determines our stature in God's eyes. Class distinctions are not recognized in the kingdom of God.

Believers are the aristocrats of heaven. There is one class only, the faith people. Faith is the Christian's coat of arms and pedigree of spiritual nobility. Paul said God has not chosen many noble, and James says he has chosen those "rich in faith and heirs of the kingdom which He promised to those who love Him" (1 Cor. 1:26; James 2:5).

There was once an unknown and unnamed woman, not all that wealthy. She perceived that Elisha was a man of God. Unbelief would have been blind to it. She made a room for Elisha and gave him hospitality. The Bible calls her a "notable woman" (2 Kings 4:8). She did not wish to be mentioned to the king or the army chief, for she was self-assured and made self-sufficient by her faith, and in that lay her greatness. She is mentioned in the Hebrews 11 roll of honor as "having obtained a good testimony through faith" (v. 39). People of faith care little for those to whom the world gives its fading honors, as Jesus said, "How can you believe, who receive honor from one another?" (John 5:44).

FAITH DEFINED

Unfortunately faith has become a religious abstraction. All faith words in Scripture come from a root that means faithfulness, reliability in relationships, acting on the trustworthiness and honesty of somebody else. Faith is accepting the credibility of God—"He who promised is faithful" (Heb. 10:23).

Make a note of this—true faith is not in things happening, but it is personal confidence in God. Faith means we leave things to Him and step out in trust.

The central Bible maxim is "Trust in the Lord," and that should be followed by the attitude "Though He slay me, yet will I trust Him" (Job 13:15). Jesus expected that kind of trust when He made that most remarkable and paradoxical statement, "They will put some of you to death. And you will be hated by all for my name's sake. But not a hair of your head shall be lost" (Luke 21:16–18).

Here are some valuable pointers to true faith:

- Faith is not merely being orthodox, or being positive about doctrine, for we can be ultra-correct but with not a scrap of real trust in God.

- To try to do a deal with God and say, "I will believe in You, God, if You answer this prayer," is gross ignorance of the whole matter. That is not trust.

- God does not always do what we think He should do. In fact, that is why we have to trust Him. If He always answered every prayer, faith would not be needed.

- We ask, "Why?", but who are we to demand to know why God does or does not do something as a condition for our trust? What sort of trust is that? It is so conditional that it fails to be faith altogether.

- God accepts no terms for trust. Must God conform to the reasonings of our puny minds on pain of being disbelieved?

- If we do not believe, it is our loss, not His.

- Faith cannot be measured except by the task undertaken in faith.

So far this chapter has dealt with faith in general. This has been absolutely necessary in order to clear the ground to talk about greater faith, or the gift of faith. The acquisition of faith is a major Bible topic. Its teaching applies as much to the gift of faith as any other form. Hebrews 11 lists the elders who obtained a good testimony all through one thing—faith. It calls them our witnesses, or spectators, as we run the faith race.

THE GIFT OF FAITH DEFINED

All faith is a gift, the work of God (John 6:29). Paul alludes to what Jesus said about faith moving mountains and links it with the gift of the Spirit in 1 Corinthians 13:2: "Though I have all faith, so that I could remove mountains…" Earlier we said that not even Jesus moved mountains by the power of faith, but we do read, "By faith we understand that the worlds were framed by the word of God, so that the things which are seen were not made of things which are visible" (Heb. 11:3). Faith is the invisible reality.

That kind of faith power is treated in Scripture as extraordinary. The gift is a manifestation of the Spirit, as we saw, and this kind of faith has all the marks of the supernatural might of God. That is the gift—faith given by an act of the Spirit. It is useless to exhort congregations to exercise faith on that level. They cannot have mountain-moving faith just by trying. Like the Welsh old lady who tried it on the mountain that blocked the view from her window. She got up the next morning, saw it was still there, and commented, "I thought as much!" Faith is not the product of striving, straining, and concentrating. It is rest, not labor.

I preached in the Entertainment Centre of Perth, Australia, which was packed with eight thousand people waiting to see a miracle. In faith I said that they would see one. I sat down on the platform and prayed, "Lord, where is the key miracle tonight?" The Holy Spirit whispered in my soul, "Look left; that lady in the wheelchair will be healed tonight." An assurance warmed me, she would be healed—that was the gift of faith.

When I stood up, I told the people what the Holy Spirit had put in my heart. I turned to the lady herself and, with everyone listening, asked her, "Madam, do you believe?"

She was frightened and buried her head in her arms. In my heart I conferred with the Lord, saying to Him, "Lord, this woman does not even believe it." The Lord replied, "It does not matter. Today it is not her faith but your faith that counts." "Thank You, Lord!" I answered.

Now the national television crew had arrived. I preached the message of salvation, then I said to the audience, "Now the moment has come. I will go and pray for that lady to be healed." I walked to her and began to pray. Then I said, "Rise in the name of Jesus." The woman looked at me as if I was crazy. Walk? Impossible! She attempted to stand but was very unstable, but I believed God, and encouraged her. "In the name of Jesus, walk!" Suddenly, the power of God shot through her very bones. She jumped forward and then ran, while eight thousand people roared in praise and wonder to God. The TV team caught the whole episode on camera.

This lady had suffered from brittleness of bones and was not expected ever to walk normally again. But what is impossible with men is possible with God. I met her two years later, still perfectly healed. What is of faith lasts forever.

THE GIFT OF FAITH
IN THE LOCAL CHURCH

When we view the exploits of men and women such as Moses and Elijah, or George Müller and Smith Wigglesworth, we may feel very small.

Yet they in themselves were not special. "Elijah was a

man with a nature like ours" (Greek: *homoiopathes*—"same feeling") (James 5:17). They were simply raised up in their times for enterprises, which obviously called for the courageous faith gift, that God granted them. Their boldness in God challenged the world.

We now come to the heart of the question. What is the gift of faith? So far as is practical we will start with a definition.

> The gift of faith is the manifestation of the Holy Spirit imparting that special faith needed for a special work that God puts before us. The work may be large or small, but faith is a gift to all those to whom it is necessary in order for them to do what they have to do.

The illustrious names of certain nation-moving and world-shaking people of faith are constantly given us. But why just these? Are they really the privileged few? The truth is, whoever does the will of God, whether in a sphere large or limited, will enjoy this same resource. If tongues and prophecy are available to us in our town or village church, why are we afflicted with a sense of inferiority that supposes other gifts are only for eminent leaders? If one gift is available, then all gifts are available, according to God's will.

WHERE THE CHURCH IS

All gifts, including the manifestation of faith, are for the local church. The Corinthian church, Paul testified, came "short in no gift" (1 Cor. 1:7). True, nobody in Corinth ever moved mountains or, by faith, plucked up trees and planted them in the sea, but the gift of faith was theirs according to their opportunities and local problems. Spiritual gifts are not the exclusive equipment of world leaders or those prominent in what we call the "wider church."

At this point, we shall have to make a digression and look at two facts. First, the word *church* simply means a gathering or congregation (Greek: *ekklesia*) and is so used in both Old and New (Greek) Testaments. It does not signify an organized, official membership, for such a thing was unknown in the New Testament. Secondly, there is no such thing in the New Testament as the church catholic, or universal. The body of Christ is always local.

At the beginning there were sometimes many churches, or congregations in houses, in one city. If they all came together, then that also would be called the church, i.e., a gathering. We speak of "the Anglican Church," but each local congregation in a city is the church. The Methodist Church is the name given to Methodists worldwide, which is a convenient term, but the actual *ekklesia* is wherever born-again Methodists meet.

There is nothing whatever in Scripture obliging all Christians in a city to belong to one church. It speaks of the church in Ephesus, or Philippi, but there are not even the flimsiest grounds to teach that we can have only one church in a town, village, or area such as Hackney or Brooklyn. If we want to do it that way, that is up to us. God does not interfere with what we organize. He gives us the wisdom to arrange our Christian fellowship with practical convenience, whether independent or denominational. The pattern was still developing when the New Testament closed.

God blesses us in all kinds of situations. When our gospel crusades are backed by all the Christian churches in a city, those congregations are the church. One day, when all believers are caught up to be with Christ forever, then that gathering to Christ will be the universal church, all one in Christ.

GIFTS FOR THE LOCAL CHURCH

Now that digression about the church was important. It tells us where the gifts of the Spirit may be manifested. When we read of the fivefold ministry of men whom Christ gives to the church, it is widely assumed that they are for the world church or for a whole group of churches. But no such universal church, or group of churches, existed when Paul was writing. When he speaks of gifts for the church, it is Christ's ideal for each individual assembly (Eph. 4:11), though the ideal is not always reached.

That is the Word of God, however much we may have to adjust our traditional thinking. The aim is to build people up to the full stature locally, blessed with all spiritual blessings and all gifts, as was the Corinthian church. While the church is simply a gathering, it is also a gathering of faithful and regular people. All the pastoral epistles assume that there are a number of recognized members who constantly meet, forming a stable assembly. Wanderers from church to church claiming they are members of the world church would be under suspicion in Paul's churches, as no church could be built at all if everybody was so fickle. Each assembly is a God-recognized spiritual entity in its own right and qualifies for the gifts whether or not it has links to other churches.

ACCORDING TO THE TASK

According to our call and sphere of service God gives us faith. We have faith for every task, whatever God wants us to undertake. We do not read that Smith Wigglesworth parted the sea like Moses, or that Moses healed the sick like Wigglesworth. We do not read that Müller brought down fire from heaven or challenged the monarch on his throne like Elijah, but Elijah did not feed two thousand orphans by faith. Each according to his place.

If mountains must be moved, there will be faith to do it, and not until then. There are leaders exercising ministries literally affecting nations. They are doing just what they are called to do—and they exercise faith for that. Not all see mighty healings—that is not their gift, but they head evangelism into half the world. Their faith-gift is conspicuous. Nevertheless, when we labor out of sight in some remote corner, the same gift will operate.

FAITH AND OBEDIENCE

The faith-gift makes all things possible. Even ordinary faith produces outstanding people, though not all church members are notable examples of its galvanizing power. Some are still at the growth stage, where they declare they would go through fire and water for God—but only if it does not rain. Paul and Silas in Philippi, sick with horribly mutilated backs, had a celebration meeting in the pitch-black prison, and then they conducted a baptismal service before they had recovered from their terrible mauling. That is not all, for we read that when they left, "they [that is Paul and Silas] encouraged them" (Acts 16:40). Paul and Silas, battered and wounded, encouraged the brethren they left there.

That is the kind of possibility that the gift of faith opens up. This is rather different from staying away from worship on Sunday in case the cold, caught in the rain at the football match on Saturday, gets worse, or to catch up with work that we did not do during the week when we were watching interesting nonsense on television, or because we feel tired. "Those who honor Me I will honor," says the Lord (1 Sam. 2:30). Believe it, and our habits will change—and our health!

Now we can learn something from the two words *faith* and *obedience*. The Greek word for "unbelief" (*apistia*) and "to be disobedient" (*apeitheo*) belong to the same root word. To obey God you need faith, but faith is given when you obey. Obedience is faith, and faith means doing what God says. Not being able to do it is no excuse, for we are able to do it, by faith. God offers us the resource of the gift of faith. Prodigies are possible. Ordinary people can expand their potential, and to that, history is witness. Jesus challenged His hearers, "What do you do more than the others?" (Matt. 5:47). If we are "faithed" by the Spirit, we can tackle the impossible.

That is the characteristic of Christianity. The hallmark of God's work in us is that He dispatches us into worlds that nobody else has ever conquered. Study the story of Peter walking on the water. Three miles out on the sea of Galilee the disciples saw Jesus gliding toward them on the water. They shrieked themselves hoarse with superstitious terror, thinking that He was a ghost. Jesus called to them, "It is I." Now Peter knew Jesus. He knew the only Person in the whole universe who would tell him to do the impossible.

That was the acid test of His identity. Peter challenged the apparition, saying, "Lord, if it is You, command me to come to You on the water" (Matt. 14:28). Jesus did challenge him. Peter walked on the waves to Christ. That was a manifestation of the gift of faith. Jesus is the one who calls men and women to be greater than they thought themselves to be. If you are thinking of following Jesus, you should know He is like that. He does not call you just to hold a lily or pick buttercups. The tongue-tied preach. Fishermen become fishers of men. Harlots become lovers of God. Cripples walk. That shows it is Jesus, the true God, who sends you to undertake what you would normally never consider.

Of course, doing what He commands also identifies the true believer and reveals the gift of faith. "For by You I can run against a troop" (Ps. 18:29). "I can do all things through Christ who strengthens me" (Phil. 4:13). Nobody has faith to move mountains until mountains need to be moved. But there is faith to do whatever God bids us do—when we do it. The size of faith is not the right language. The necessary size of the tool of faith will be handed out to us according to the size of the job.

FORMULA FAITH

To speak and make a positive "confession" in faith is obviously an excellent practice. Positive language helps positive attitudes. However, we must not turn this into a doctrine, for it is not in the Bible. The secret of getting God to do things does not lie merely in saying the right thing, getting the formula right, or in positive talk. It is alarming to suggest that God can be made to act if we only speak with the proper technique, that saying it makes God do it. If it seemed so— and there are always testimonies to anything—then those concerned also had faith in their hearts, which was the actual cause. Faith activates the miraculous. That is the dynamic. David's challenge to Goliath has been used as an example illustrating how victory comes through positive confession. What is not mentioned is that Goliath also spoke a positive confession—and lost! No amount of positive shouting will deceive God if we are not acting in obedience and trust in Him and do not believe "in our heart," as Jesus said.

There are ample Bible instances that do not fit this "miracle in your mouth" formula. David, in fact, confessed negatively—"I shall perish someday by the hand of Saul" (1 Sam. 27:1)—but he did not, as you know!

However, our object is not merely to comment on formula faith but to show that it is faith that operates, whatever shape it comes in. Those proclaiming their discoveries and innovations back them up with many testimonies. No doubt, but it is not the techniques and teachings that succeed, but it is the underlying faith in God. God cannot be made to jump when we press the right button and say the right thing, but God does honor faith, even when it comes larded over with peculiar ideas. As articulate beings we must articulate our faith, but whatever the words in our mouth, or the nonsense in our head, God sees only what is in our heart.

> Faith, mighty faith, the promise sees
> And looks to that alone;
> Laughs at impossibilities,
> And cries, "It shall be done!"[2]

CHAPTER 10

HEALING, PART 1

THE GIFT OF healing draws the greatest interest, and so we must give it very careful attention. It embraces so many divergent views—many nonscriptural. Some want to disprove it, and others have extreme views saying we need never be sick or even die. The subject is a minefield, but we will plot a course by the Word of God, first about healing in general and then about gifts of healings.

WHY GOD HEALS

Healing, as we shall explain it here, began with Jesus. There had always been superstitions, of course, prayers to the gods, healing waters such as we read of in John chapter 5, and so on, just as in the world today. Those bitten by snakes were healed as they believed and looked on the serpent of brass made by Moses, which Jesus Himself referred to in John 3:14. However, the healing ministry of Christ was totally new and startling, and, for that matter, so is the ministry of Christ today through His believing churches.

What Jesus did gives us some fundamental truths.

Jesus healed without any condition or pressing people to be converted. Of course He did seek the lost people of His day, as He does those of our day, but whether they believed that He was the Son of God or not, He healed them. His compassion was unhesitating and universal. When a foreign soldier said his servant was sick, Jesus immediately said, "I will come and heal him" (Matt. 8:7). His work among the sick was a demonstration of the truth of divine grace.

Jesus acted in the name of God the Father and so demonstrated the truth that health is the normal blessing of God, like the sun and the rain for the just and unjust. He healed without obligation, for love, not for effect, because the sick were sick.

Christ did not just love souls, but He also loved people. He had concern for their physical needs. God loved the world (Greek: *kosmos*, the inhabited globe), all His creatures, so that not a sparrow falls from the housetop without the Father knowing, Jesus said. By healing the afflicted, Jesus asserted that He was doing the Father's work and showing what God's attitude really is toward everything that breathes.

Jesus's whole ministry was more than physical cures. He said, in every way possible, that the whole man needed help—physical, psychological, and spiritual. He wanted to do far more than heal, saying that it was not useful for a

man to be sound in body if he went into hellfire. He was disappointed when people went away too easily content. "You
only come to me for bread that perishes, not for the bread of
heaven that gives you everlasting life," He sadly told them.
(See John 6:26–27.) He wanted them to read His wonders
as signs, spelling out the tremendous truth of a vast heart
of love that was beating for them—that they needed God.
Often people accepted the handout of a cure but turned away,
and they stayed outside the comprehensive benefits of the
kingdom of God.

Jesus was not a mere social reformer. His method was
intensely personal and concerned with the entire personality.
The point of the healing of the woman with a hemorrhage
is not so much the healing itself as His personal concern for
her. Ringed by a peering crowd, He calmed her fears and
assured her of salvation. She had taken healing from His
robe, but He could not just let it go at that. He wanted it to
be personal, so everybody would know that it was a love gift
from Him to her.

Christ sought to create a relationship of praise, thankful-
ness, and worship between the sick and His Father. When
He healed the blind man (John 9), Jesus went to find him
afterward and asked him, "Do you believe in the Son of
God?" The episode ends with this: "Then he [the man]
said, 'Lord, I believe!' And he worshiped Him" (v. 38). Jesus
instructed the disciples to heal the sick, and then, beyond
that, they must proclaim the real good news, the gospel, that

"the kingdom of God has come near to you" (Luke 10:9). He healed the leper (Mark 1:41–45) and sent him to offer a sacrifice of thanksgiving as a testimony. He also healed ten lepers, but only one, a Samaritan, came back to thank Him (Luke 17:12–19). Jesus remarked, "Where are the nine? Were there not any found who returned to give glory to God except this foreigner?" (vv. 17–18). He wanted those healed to have more, to establish a relationship of worship with God.

Even in the beginning Moses said to Pharaoh, "Thus says the LORD God of Israel: 'Let My people go, that they may hold a feast to Me in the wilderness'" (Exod. 5:1). Pharaoh did not question it. Israel was released for God's praise in the earth, and their song of praise is recorded over and over throughout Scripture.

Jesus gave people deliverance often before they turned to God, even if they failed to do so nine times out of ten—a fair average perhaps in our gospel meetings. Healing may be an end in itself—if that is all we want. But from God's angle, it is to open our hearts to more love.

Here is an all-important summary to be well learned. To know and love God is more important than healing. Many go unhealed despite prayer and faith, but healing is not everything. Sickness is not the ultimate evil, nor are cures the ultimate good.

It is absurd to lose faith when healing does not come. God does far more than heal, and He does not fail. There are infinitely higher benefits for which Christ labored and died. Healing, in fact, only takes on meaning, significance, and value when it opens a soul to the love of God. Then it becomes a sign they have read.

HEALERS WHO SUFFER

There is a strange background to healing. "By His stripes we are healed"—that verse in Isaiah 53:5 we know well enough, but it has a neglected dimension. Those who go with Christ to heal will know something of His stripes. He sends out those who are ready to suffer. Jesus sent out His disciples to heal the sick and, at the same time, warned them that they were called upon to suffer and be persecuted. Healing and cross-bearing go together. They may even suffer sickness, as Paul apparently did, as he told the Corinthians. At least any firsthand experience generates sympathy with the afflicted. Healing and suffering are destined to go hand in hand. Somebody suffers, whoever is healed.

Perhaps you want a healing ministry? Then, alongside the glory, be prepared for tears, heartache, disappointment, frustration, and persecution. The price for others' wholeness was Christ's brokenness. Those who minister His grace best will share something of Christ's inner heart. There is also the completely irrational attitude of the world. Those who pray for the sick will be attacked. The world will make those suffer who bring divine relief for suffering. There are men who write clever books against divine healing and who never lift a finger to bring relief to any sufferer.

THE PROBLEM OF THE UNHEALED

If you want the gift of healing, you will certainly come up against the question of suffering. What do you say when prayer for the sick seems unanswered? In fact, this question is bound up with what we have been saying: that Jesus heals because He suffered. I need to explain that. Remember that what Jesus was, He is—the same yesterday, today, and forever. What Jesus was on the cross, He is on the throne—the Lamb slain from the foundation of the earth. He never changes and is the eternal God. God heals because He suffers.

If God suffers, what a world of truth that opens up! It is as if He took the responsibility for all the evil in the world. He accepts it into His own infinite experience. He carries our sorrows. He cares for us. He absorbed the tragedy of the Fall into His own being. He took the shrieking discords of sin and misery and wrote them into the score of the eternal symphony of love—the everlasting sounds of heaven, the minor mode of the eternal music of His being. But that same truth gives us the most powerful hope of His healing. Wherever He can, He relieves the oppressed and delivers the afflicted.

However, no Christian should sit down and fatalistically accept sickness—either his own or anybody else's—as the incomprehensible will of God, because our God is not incomprehensible. We wage war against sickness, since it is a mark of evil, and although we cannot make a wholesale end of it and cure everybody in sight, that is no reason why people should not be healed.

HEALINGS BELONG TO THE KINGDOM

Next there is an issue upon which we must make the most careful distinction. Miracles do authenticate the gospel, but that is not the reason for miracles. It is a gross error, in fact, to suppose that God heals the sick just to prove something or establish something. If that was the object, then lack of healing would have the opposite effect and would disprove Christianity. But, in fact, when the sick stay sick, it disproves nothing.

One form of this error comes from the school of thought that says healings were only temporary for the beginning of the church in order to establish it. It really is a shocking and scandalous suggestion. Is God like that? Healing the sick not for their sake, but for His private interests? Did God really use afflicted people just as a convenient opportunity to work a few miracles until Christianity was well established, just like fire starters, and then show no practical interest in them any longer? Is that love? Or heartlessness?

We have said elsewhere that Paul's reference to the *charismata* in 1 Corinthians 12 is part of his doctrine of the church; that is, the gifts are a basic feature of the church. Nowhere is there the slightest suggestion that what was built into the church has now been taken out.

It was certainly part of the original truth. The early church preached a Christ who healed, and that is how the evange-lists proclaimed Him in Matthew, Mark, Luke, and John. What right has anybody to preach a Christ who does not heal, if they preach the Christ of the four Gospels?

If God did not intend this mercy to be extended to our times, we certainly do not get that impression by reading Scripture. At least there is no statement that makes it at all clear. On the contrary, every statement assumes that Christ never changes and continues the work He began.

Jesus sent the disciples to proclaim the kingdom of God. Miracles of healing were the evidences of the power of that kingdom. Where is the kingdom without that evidence? For centuries the church lacked such genuine power-signs. Instead it transferred the whole idea of the kingdom into the temporal authority of the church, turning the kingdom into an empire that limited kings and kingdoms through the pope of Rome. This followed Augustine's book *The City of God*.

If we deny miracles, as many did and do, whether liberals or even evangelicals, we change the character of the gospel we preach. A non-miracle gospel is reduced to a purely spiritual religion, ineffective on earth. If we do that, then somehow we are left with the necessity of making such a heavenly teaching relevant, for it pretty well ceases to be so for people walking around in shoes on earth. The real gospel needs nobody to show it to be relevant—it just is. The baker never yet had to argue that his shop is "relevant." The gospel is the bread of life, bringing life and healing to mind, body, and soul—preach it, and all the world sees that it matters.

The kingdom of God has been introduced on earth, and healing shows it; unless it continues that way, how do we know it is the same gospel? The gospel witnesses to itself by signs following. Without healing it is stripped of a powerful element of its self-authentication. Healing is not detachable; it's not a mere bit of gadgetry or an accessory. It is integral to the gospel.

Do we really preach Christ? Yes? Then Matthew shows that wherever Jesus went, when He moved from one place to another, He always healed. It was a consistent habit of Christ. Peter also said that healing is what He went about doing. That is Jesus!

THE GIFT

Now we come to "the gifts of healings." The gift of healing is not mentioned in the Bible. It is a useful term but unfortunately has been appropriated by spiritualist healers, psychics, New Agers, and others. Christians were using it, however, long before the modern "healing epidemic" (as somebody called it) began.

Paul always uses the plural expression "gifts of healings." It comes three times in 1 Corinthians 12:9, 28, 30. These plural gifts are from one person to another; that is, many healings through one individual, acting as a steward, for healings to be given to the needy and afflicted. If we put the context of this gift together with it, we would read, "To another is given the manifestation of the gifts of healings," or in more common terms, "the gift of the gifts of healings." This is not a commission to heal all and sundry, but only such as the Holy Spirit gives a manifestation for.

HEALING WORDS

Let us look carefully at the words for "healing" originally found in the New Testament. Here in 1 Corinthians 12:9 it is "physical cures" (Greek: *iama*, from *iaomai*). It is not used for anything else, except metaphorically a couple of times. This is the ordinary word for medical recoveries. Luke, "the beloved physician," uses the root word *iaomai* the most: seventeen times.

Two other words are the Greek *sozo* and *diasozo*, which occur ninety-seven times, translated "to heal" fourteen times. Its best equivalent in English is "to make whole, to make well," whether spiritually or physically, as in Mark 6:56—"As many as touched Him were made well." *Sozo* was used by the Greeks when writing to their friends enquiring about their health.

It is a fundamental fact that, as human beings, we are not only flesh but also spirit. The two are inextricably joined, and to know what is of the body and what is of the spirit is often impossible. The Bible teaching on this bond is not a side issue, but it lies at the core of scriptural revelation, including the whole issue of salvation. Any theology that tries to divide the benefits of salvation between body and soul is bound to be artificial.

That is how early Christian fathers viewed it. Irenaeus, the disciple of Polycarp, who knew the apostle John, declared in *Against the Heresies* that the body is capable of salvation. Justin Martyr, who died in A.D. 165, also declared that God saves man, not part of a man, not his soul alone, but the body also.

Another term is used in Mark 16:18: "They will lay hands on the sick, and they will recover." The phrase "will recover" here is literally "get well" (Greek: *kalos echo*), a process of recuperation.

Four different words are used in Luke 17:11–19 for the healing of the ten lepers: mercy, cleansing, cure, and healing (Greek: *eleeo*—have pity; *katharizo*—was cleaned; *iaomai*—was cured; *sozo*—has healed). These are also salvation words, but they are certainly used for physical deliverance here.

The most frequent term for healing in the New Testament is "therapy" (Greek: *therapeia, therapeuo*), occurring forty-five times. It relates to the process or means of cure.

Now it has been said that there are no gradual cures in the New Testament. In fact, not one of the Greek words quoted above suggests instant recovery. For example, a gradual work is indicated in the case of the ten lepers. They were healed "as they went." They were going from Galilee to Jerusalem, which would take two or three days. What we know of any Old Testament cures is that they were gradual recoveries. We know some cures were immediate, but only because we are explicitly told. In Mark's Gospel "immediately" is a favorite expression for other actions besides healing. Peter was an "immediate" sort of man and is thought to be the source for Mark's Gospel. Immediate healing impressed him. Instant recoveries are far more memorable. That is also the case today.

The Old Testament has no equivalent Hebrew word for the English word *health*. Not to be ill was taken as the natural state. Sickness was considered to be a withdrawal of natural life by God. This stems from Genesis 2:17: "Of the tree of the knowledge of good and evil you shall not eat, for in the day that you eat of it you shall surely die."

Sin brought about loss of vitality and the beginning of death. All recovery was taken as forgiveness. The restored favor of God restored the life energy from God, which normally sustained everybody, saving people from death. Diseases and plagues represented the curse of God. They exhausted human life forces, leading to silence and inactivity in the grave, where praise to God ends.

That was the general teaching before Christ. Typical of this is Psalm 103:1–5. "Bless the LORD, O my soul…who forgives all your iniquities, who heals all your diseases, who redeems your life from destruction" (vv. 2–4). It goes on contrasting "the pit" with a return to youthful vigor—"your youth is renewed like the eagle's" (v. 5). Healing and forgiveness are invariably spoken of together in the Old Testament. Psalm 32:1–5 is typical.

King Asa, in 2 Chronicles 16:12, turned to the doctors instead of seeking God. This has been grossly misunderstood. It is not a condemnation of doctors. It has been taken as the grounds for saying that believers should not go to doctors. Scripture does not speak against medical doctors. The real explanation is that King Asa had sinned and believed that was why he was sick. However, instead of repenting and seeking forgiveness first in order to be healed, as he very well knew he should, he asked the doctors to cure him, to outwit God, as it were, and to get him well without repentance or forgiveness.

MORE LIGHT

In the New Testament the Lord brings us far more light. He changes or qualifies the idea that if a person suffers, they must personally be guilty and deserving of judgment (though we all are). It was that idea that caused so much puzzlement to Job and his friends and to the writers of many psalms, such as Psalm 37 and Psalm 73. He still keeps before us the fact that sin and suffering are linked and that hell awaits sinners, but He also recognizes that the innocent suffer.

Jesus shows particular concern for the victims of other people's wickedness—the struggle of fathers and mothers, the distress of children, the bereaved, the frightened, the demon driven, the unwanted and outcasts, the hungry, the untouchables, refugees—all those who had done nothing to deserve such miseries. The sick came to Him like an endless river. They touched His heart, and over them He shed tears and, finally, His blood. He championed the cause of all sufferers. To offend one of His little ones (we are all His little ones, incidentally), He said, would bring such woe upon the offenders' own heads that to be dropped in the sea with a millstone around their necks would be more pleasant.

To understand sickness, we have to learn that there is a universal disturbance of the order of God to which we all contribute. Personal sin makes us more vulnerable to the prevailing conditions of evil, so that a sickness could well be linked with our own failure. In Christ's day the sad masses believed afflictions branded them as sinful. This added to their distress. Jesus showed them that He was forgiving and caring. Guilt could be lifted from their consciences to give them the peace of heaven in their soul.

When He said, "I have come that [you] may have life," they understood it, better than many today, as meaning life for body and soul. He told a paralyzed man he was forgiven and told the disciples, "Peace [shalom] I leave with you," that is, well-being and prosperity. The congregation in the Nazareth synagogue (Luke 4) would clearly understand that healing was intended when Jesus spoke from Isaiah 61:1–2, especially when He used the specific illustration of the healing of Naaman the leper.

Sometimes mistaken theology produces a mistaken translation of the Bible. One we ought to correct is John 9. Seeing a blind man, the disciples began to philosophize, asking who had sinned—his parents or himself—before he was born (as if he could!). Jesus said, "Neither!" Wrong punctuation of verse 3 has disguised what Jesus did. "Neither this man nor his parents sinned, but that the works of God should be revealed in him." That surely amounts to a slander upon God. Jesus used the imperative: "Let the work of God be done!" The Greek uses no causal term. It does not suggest that the man was born blind in order to be healed. Correctly it should read: "This man has not sinned, nor his parents, but let the work of God be done in him. I must work the work of God while I am in the world." In other words, the work of God was not to make people blind but to give them sight. God made eyes from clay at Creation, and Jesus repeated the process for this blind man. "I must work the works of Him who sent me while it is day," Christ said (v. 4). Jesus was doing what the Father did, and then He added, "As long as I am in the world, I am the light of the world.... For judgment I have come into this world, that those who do not see may see" (vv. 5, 39). John chapter 9 is put there to show that God does not inflict people or cure them just to make a point.

CHAPTER 11

HEALING, PART 2

N OW WE ARE ready to tackle the phrase "gifts of healings"; that is, multiple gifts for multiple sicknesses. So many guesses have been applied to it, particularly that it means one person can heal one thing and another person heal something else—one the blind, another the deaf, and so on.

Some have interpreted the gift by their experience, which is always an unsafe procedure. They have found one particular affliction being cured, or cured more than other troubles, and they have taken that to mean that they have "found their gift," as they say. One spoke of himself as an "arthritis specialist." Leg-lengthening, plus perhaps the claim of a "discernment" to detect sufferers from a short limb, is another specialist healing claim. God does adjust limbs, of course, but this "gift" is, incidentally, open to question. Measuring a leg is notoriously difficult, even for medical professionals. An imperceptible movement of the hip, made even involuntarily, can produce the impression of a limb growing. This kind of healing is suspiciously like a technique rather than a miracle. Onlookers sometimes wonder whose leg is being pulled!

In Scripture nobody specialized in one affliction. Like salvation, healing is to the "whosoever." A single-affliction gift—for deafness, say, but not for heart trouble—would be discrimination. An evangelist would never offer God's forgiveness for theft but not for adultery. Our faith should rest on God, not healing; nor should it be limited to what we have seen God heal. If we see only one sickness cured and believe only for that, it is all we will ever see. It is time to get back to the Word.

Jesus healed "all kinds of sickness and all kinds of disease among the people" (Matt. 4:23), and Peter did likewise. People brought to him "sick people and those who were tormented by unclean spirits, and they were all healed" (Acts 5:16). Through the apostles' hands "many signs and wonders were done among the people" (v. 12). We read how, when Paul was on the Isle of Malta, "the rest of those on the island who had diseases also came and were healed" (Acts 28:9). A gift of healing for one specific affliction only has no Bible precedent.

BUILDING UP HOPES?

If you pray for the sick, you will find accusations being made that you are heartless, building up hopes and sending some home unhealed. Following my Fire Conference in Frankfurt, some German clergy were reported in the press as making this kind of allegation. The fact that countless people were healed apparently should not have happened, in case others were not healed! It is hard to understand this kind of mentality, which supposes it is a higher virtue to heal nobody than to heal only a few hundred. I know many German clergy who practice on this high moral ground, showing compassion on the sick by not praying for any of them! I am sure they disappoint one person—the Lord Jesus Christ Himself.

One woman was carried onto the Frankfurt platform with a few days to live. She was dying with cancer. In front of eight thousand people God gave me the key miracle that He had promised and raised her up. If her cure cost others dashed hopes (which is not true), we must leave that to God.

If anybody thinks that we ought not to build up people's hopes in case they are not healed, they had better advise the afflicted never to open their Bibles. The Word of God is, without doubt, the worst offender in building up expectations! In fact I, like most of my colleagues, would never have laid hands on anybody without Bible warrant, and mainly we have been inspired directly by the Word of God to do so.

Of course, some deny that the Bible teaches healing, just as some deny that it says that Jesus is the Son of God. There is no Christian doctrine taught in the Scriptures that is not denied by some group. I find, however, that it needs a good deal of sophisticated and complicated exposition of the Word not to preach divine healing. It is such a straightforward truth. The golden rule of Bible interpretation is that usually the simple explanation is the most likely one, even in difficult passages. On the very surface, healing is a Bible truth. Healing passages are not even difficult, except when turned into controversy—the common strategy of those who do not believe what the Bible really says.

All this is exemplified in the healing of Mrs. Jean Neil of Rugby, England. It stirred up an angry reaction from one or two whose pet theories were challenged. She had suffered twenty-five years of physical trouble, sometimes getting better but then being thrown back again, as when she was in a car crash and her spine was damaged. One day she had a dream so vivid she could remember every detail. She saw herself in a very large building and a man coming first to another woman in a wheelchair and then over to her.

For nearly two years she had more or less lived in a wheelchair. She might hobble a few steps by twisting from side to side, as one limb was dislocated at the hip. She had worn a special medical corset to accommodate the distortion. Drugs had affected color coordination in her eyes; she had had heart attacks, which left her with angina; and her spine had already been surgically fused and the coccyx removed. She suffered excruciating pain and sometimes screamed as she moved. Various specialists had treated her in hospitals. At that time she was having to decide whether to undergo another critical and expensive operation on her spine. The surgeon said it could leave her worse or bring her not more than a degree of relief. Jean also had bronchitis, asthma, and a hiatus hernia.

One day, a short time after her dream, she was taken with her husband to a rally in the Birmingham (England) National Exhibition Centre. She looked round and recognized the place of her dream. Some eleven thousand people were present and heard my salvation message. Afterward I went to minister to the sick and laid my hands first upon a wheelchair patient. Then God spoke to me and directed me right across this vast hall to minister to a woman at the side aisle—Mrs. Neil. I prayed, told her to stand—which, uncertainly, she did—and then suddenly, as she described it later, a great force went through her system. Within two minutes she had abandoned the confinement of her wheelchair forever and was literally running round the place, jumping as if she had never had anything wrong with her. Every ailment in her body had instantly vanished.

Mrs. Neil has since traveled thousands of miles testifying to God's goodness. She took up jogging and swimming, and today she is a fit woman who never feels a single spasm of pain. The greatness of this miracle is seen in that although part of the spine had been surgically fused, and the work still shows on X-ray, the specialist under whose care she was could find no impairment whatever of her movements. Total function has been restored.

One of the objections that arose from this cure was that we had published her story. It was asserted that if God works a miracle, we must not testify about it in case it gives false hope to sufferers from similar afflictions. Well, the Bible itself strongly encourages testimony: "Let the redeemed of the LORD say so" (Ps. 107:2). Scripture largely consists of testimony to the greatness of the works of God, and the intention is also clear—to encourage us to believe that the God of yesterday will do the same things today. The most positive grounds are laid down in countless passages that "the truth of the LORD endures forever" (Ps. 117:2).

CRITICISM OF CHRIST

It is disobedience to Christ not to minister healing. To raise the objection that not all are healed is a criticism of Jesus who commanded us to heal. He Himself delivered some but passed by others, and He does the same now through His church. Critics overlook something. Healing is only a part or aspect of the responsibility to bring our petitions to God. Not all prayers are answered. There is no difference between asking for one thing and asking for another. If people do not pray for the sick because they may not be healed, are they going to be consistent and pray for nobody in any kind of trouble in case nothing happens? Should we never ask God for anything so that nobody's hopes will be dashed? If you believe nothing, then you will not be disappointed.

In Western conditions miracles are miracles because of the

prevailing winds of withering unbelief. Some entire nations are like Nazareth, where Jesus could do no mighty work.

When in my meetings the sick are healed, I hear people say, "Jesus is wonderful." When in my meetings the sick are not healed, I hear some say, "Bonnke is no good"—and I agree with them. If there is a fault, it may be either mine or theirs, but Jesus never fails.

THE GIFT AND THE GIFTS

Now we must come back to the phrase "gifts of healings." We will ask a question first, and that will lead us to a full explanation of the gift. Does it mean there are just so many healings earmarked for patients? No. First, we remember that God shows no partiality (Acts 10:34). James, brought up with Jesus as part of the family, was particularly impressed by Christ's undiscriminating concern, and he says, "Do not hold the faith…with partiality…but if you show partiality, you commit sin, and are convicted by the law as transgressors" (James 2:1, 9). This was part of the "royal law" of the kingdom (vv. 5, 8), that we love our neighbor as ourselves. It is called the "royal law" because the King Himself acts on that principle.

Who then will receive their healing? James helps us. "Has God not chosen the poor of this world to be rich in faith and heirs of the kingdom?" (v. 5). Christ stressed the fact to John the Baptist that "the poor have the gospel preached to them" (Matt. 11:5). In Acts 3:1–8 Peter gave a gift of healing, saying to a cripple, "Silver and gold I do not have, but what I do have I give you: In the name of Jesus Christ of Nazareth, rise up and walk" (v. 6).

THE DISENFRANCHISED

Jesus had a profound feeling for the poor, but they were not the only deprived ones. Certainly Zacchaeus and other tax gatherers were rich. When Jesus preached in the synagogue at Nazareth, He built up a picture of physical deliverance for people who were deprived because they were foreigners. He referred to a non-Jewish widow outside the territory of Israel to whom God sent the prophet Elijah. Jesus then went to the same Gentile area, Sidon, to another non-Jewish woman and brought healing into her home. Sidon had its own patron god of healing, Eshmon and his temple, but he could do nothing for this woman whose daughter had a devil (Mark 7:24–30). She heard that Jesus was there, and she determined to see him. The disciples tried to get rid of her, and even Jesus tested her, but she persisted until He eventually responded.

Christ's remark is famous: "Let the children be filled first, for it is not good to take the children's bread and throw it to the little dogs" (v. 27). He describes people with rights and those without. The children were Israel, who had "rights." To them belonged the promises and the covenant of God. The "dogs" were those outside the commonwealth of Israel.

To the children of the household bread is a right, their birthright. To those outside the household it is a gift, "tossed" to them as a favor. Jesus said that healing was the bread of the children of Israel. The woman quickly realized that what was not hers by right she could have as a gift, and she wittily summed it up: "Then let some crumbs of Israel's healing bread be tossed to those of us whom they call dogs." For her background and semi-heathenism she displayed a grasp of God's universal goodness, which is comparatively rare even two thousand years later.

Early evangelists used to hammer at their hearers, saying that if they wished to be healed, they must first be saved from sin. They were both right and wrong. If people wished to come under the promises of healing, then they must be saved. But they could be healed through the gifts of healings if they were not born-again children of God—if God willed it, and if they could take the healing by the hand of faith. It rested on the graciousness of God.

It has seemed sometimes that the unsaved are healed when believers are not. This could be, and Jesus commented on this. He declared that people would come from the east and west and sit down with Father Abraham, while the children of the kingdom would be cast out. Believers can be unbelieving. Pastors explain the lack of healings under their ministry in terms that build up no expectation.

A sermon on "Six Reasons Why the Sick Are Not Healed" will not bring a line of expectant sick folk to the front. Negative teaching, sin, or rank disobedience to the will of God calls for repentance first. Meanwhile, non-Christians with a simple outlook benefit by the gifts of healings. One thing is possible, namely that God in His goodness initiates miracles to encourage faith—that is Bible teaching. So He may use the gifts of healings to help believers who may somehow have become bogged down in a non-faith situation.

THE WORD AND HEALING

Now look at the relation of the Word to healing. While Jesus did speak of healing as bread, He also spoke of the Word of God as bread. Healing is the Word of God in action! He taught us to pray, "Give us this day our daily bread." He also said, "Do not labor for the food which perishes, but for the food which endures to everlasting life" (John 6:27)—that is the Word of God. We need that bread daily. It is the life-giving, healthful, and healing Word of life. "Your word has given me life" (Ps. 119:50). "He sent His word and healed them" (Ps. 107:20). To those living daily by the bread of life, the bread of healing is no gift, but it is health imparted daily through their spiritual nutriment.

In my campaigns I do not preach healing; I preach the Word of God, and it releases living faith. It is easy then for the Holy Spirit to move through a crowd and touch people with open hearts. "Seek first the kingdom of God...and all these things shall be added" (Matt. 6:33).

If we live by the Word, we shall find life in it. God said, "Man shall not live by bread alone, but by every word that proceeds from the mouth of God" (Matt. 4:4). Withdrawal of life is reversed by the Word of life. "Every word" is not just a mouthful daily but a good meal. The multitudes that Christ fed with common bread did not pay a penny—no offering baskets went round. Jesus had said, "You give them something to eat," and that is exactly what the disciples did. The bread multiplied miraculously in their hands as they moved around supplying the people. The church is commanded, "You give them something to eat"—the Word of God, for in that Word is health and life.

A believer may be sick through sin, as we read in 1 Corinthians 11. Sin blocks the life flow, appetite for the bread of life declines, and some suffer from spiritual anorexia— "He…sent leanness into their soul" (Ps. 106:15). If the elders of the church attend upon such a person, their prayer of faith saves the sick (James 5:14–16). Those who have sinned and languish, as if cut off from the rights of the kingdom of God, can be healed and forgiven. That healing is a gift to them to restore them to full kingdom privileges.

THE ATTACK ON HEALING

All those who pray for the sick, either privately or publicly, will be offered as much discouragement as help. Unbelievers try to explain away healings. They have a few glib ways round them, and the same arguments pop up time and time again. Either the patients were not sick, or they were wrongly diagnosed, or else they suffered only from a psychosomatic ailment.

Let us face the fact that in a universe like ours, it is ridiculous to say that God cannot heal the sick. How does anybody know He cannot? Our knowledge is so limited. "My own suspicion," says atheist scientist J. B. S. Haldane, "is that the universe is not only queerer than we suppose, but queerer than we can suppose."[1] We would have to know everything about it to know what cannot happen. We cannot adopt a pose of infallibility, but there are individuals who make it their duty to inform mankind of their dogmas. However, God does know everything, and He finds miracles quite possible.

There is a curious state of mind among unbelievers. When a miracle healing takes place, they say God could not have done it because it breaks the scientific laws. They believe in "mind over matter" and psychological processes. Can mind over matter break scientific laws and God cannot? Can we believe in psychological omnipotence but not in divine omnipotence? God can do anything I believe, except fail.

Some of the healings commonly being seen as a result of prayer are very hard to parallel by other means, including psychiatric and hypnotic cures, which are notoriously unstable anyway. Nothing known in medical history equals some of the amazing happenings in our crusades and in churches worldwide, including the healing of congenital disorders, those born blind, crippled, deaf, the diseased, and those cruelly affected by accidents.

One thing I know: nobody has found one positive

statement in Scripture against divine healing. Instead, critics have had to turn to church history to claim that miracles ceased with the apostles. There are Christians who claim the Bible as their sole authority, yet to prove their doctrine that Jesus no longer heals, they refer to church history.

The universal problem of suffering will be completely solved according to Revelation 21:4—"And God will wipe away every tear from their eyes; there shall be no more death, nor sorrow, nor crying. There shall be no more pain, for the former things have passed away." We are not living in the millennium yet, or in an ideal world, for that is the great end toward which God is working out His purposes. Meanwhile the whole creation groans together waiting for that age to come, as we read in Romans chapter 8.

However, bursts of glory from that coming day light up the sky like lightning. The Holy Spirit is working with the church as once He worked with Jesus. Each healing is like a laser beam cutting through the darkness of this world, until the day dawns and Christ shall reign. Until then—what? We fight the good fight of faith, aided by the mercy of God and the gift of the gifts of healings.

CHAPTER 12

MIRACLES

W E MUST NOT assume that the "working of miracles" is more miraculous than the other eight gifts in 1 Corinthians 12. They are all the manifestation of the Spirit. Of course, the rationalizing critics dismiss the idea that any of them are supernatural, and they regard them as natural talents. What "talent" the working of miracles represents calls for an awful lot of juggling. If the miraculous is rejected, this chapter becomes an impenetrable mystery. The efforts of rationalistic scholars to produce a non-supernatural Christianity have produced something that bears no more resemblance than a rag doll to the palpitating energy and life of the gospel that carried the apostles into the pagan world two thousand years ago.

To get into this subject, I feel it would help greatly to think first about the challenging and thrilling references to the miracle power of God at work everywhere the gospel went.

The New Testament is a miracle book, and Christianity is a miracle faith. The "working of miracles" is mentioned three times in 1 Corinthians 12—verses 10, 28, and 29.

Jesus is the "captain of our faith." He lamented over Capernaum, which had not repented, despite His "mighty works," using the term three times (Matt. 11:20–23). Matthew 7:22 refers to "wonders." Reports of His "mighty works" astonished the people of Nazareth. Peter could remind the Jews that Christ had been "attested by God to you by miracles [*dunamis*], wonders [*teras*], and signs [*semeion*]" (Acts 2:22). The miracles under the hand of Philip amazed Simon the sorcerer in Samaria (Acts 8:6). It happened everywhere, such as in Galatia where there was the working of miracles, and the scattered Hebrew Christians had "tasted...the powers [miracles] of the age to come" (Heb. 6:5), "God also bearing witness both with signs and wonders, and with various miracles, and gifts of the Holy Spirit" (Heb. 2:4).

The Old Testament congregation of Israel, the "church in the wilderness," came into existence by prophetic miracle and was maintained supernaturally. Even then, with all the wonders of Exodus, it is only a picture of the church of Christ Jesus, created, as it were, from the wounded side of the Redeemer and born of God to be endowed with the same Spirit of the ancient prophets. As Israel was led by the pillar of fire and cloud, the church moves in the Spirit.

WHAT ARE MIRACLES?

Whatever miracles may be, we must first understand the word *miracle* itself. The Bible phrase is more correctly "powerful deeds" (*energemata dunameon*). It is a key word, occurring some one hundred twenty times or so in the New Testament.[1] The Christian faith is all miracle, and any representation of it without the power of the Holy Spirit is a corpse.

In many cases we read of "mighty deeds" without any more details. The disciples were never sent out without adequate divine power, not even when Jesus was on earth (Matt. 10:1). Before He left them to ascend to glory, Jesus told them not to leave Jerusalem until they were endued with power (*dunamis*) from on high (Luke 24:49), which they were (Acts 2:4). From that hour they always went with perfect assurance that they moved in the might of God. Paul said, "I know that when I come to you, I shall come in the fullness of the blessing of the gospel of Christ" (Rom. 15:29).

Generally, "mighty deeds" were healings and deliverance. "The multitudes with one accord heeded the things spoken by Philip, hearing and seeing the miracles which he did. For unclean spirits, crying with a loud voice, came out of many who were possessed; and many who were paralyzed and lame were healed.... [Simon] was amazed, seeing the miracles and signs which were done" (Acts 8:6–7, 13).

Two other Bible words to consider are authority (*exousia*)

and power (*dunamis*). Christian authority rests on power. The authority of the police, for example, would mean nothing unless backed by all the power of the state. Christ showed that He had the authority (*exousia*) on earth to forgive sins, but behind it was the power of redemption and His work on the cross, as we sing—"There is power, power, wonder-working power, in the blood of the Lamb."[2] This we shall see has a very important link with the gift of the working of miracles.

The phrase "the working of miracles" in 1 Corinthians 12:10 is literally the "operations of powers" (*energema dunamis*). It covers all varieties of signs and wonders, is plural for multiple miracles, and does not specify one particular type of miracle.

In the Old Testament miracles are mainly nature miracles, such as the plagues of Egypt, the crossing of the Red Sea, the miracles of Elijah and Elisha, and the moving of the sundial shadow in Isaiah. In the New Testament Jesus alone did such things, turning water to wine, feeding thousands with a boy's luncheon, quelling the threat of the storm, and so on. We are not told that the apostles themselves did any of these things. Healings of the sick and exorcisms were the main signs referred to as "mighty wonders."

We will dig a bit deeper. The English word *miracle* seems to convey more to the average person than what the Bible says. Many take "miracle" to mean sheer fairy-tale magic, squaring the circle, or making two plus two equal five—nonsense events. It is from the Latin word *miraculum*, meaning to wonder at, that we get the English word *miracle*. It relates more to the magic of mythology than Christianity. Too often English-speaking people think of a miracle as that kind of thing, putting the Bible on the same level as mythology.

Whatever God has done in creation or may do in His sovereign omnipotence, the promise of the baptism with the Spirit does not copy myths, but what Scripture portrays. H. G. Wells's famous story "The Man Who Could Work Miracles" describes how he first made a candle float upside down, and the flame burn downward, and then went on to destroy the earth with his "faith." Christianity has nothing in common with fairy-tale fantasy. Everything that Christ did and everything that the gifts enable us to do are all in line with divine and moral purpose, reflecting God's wisdom.

There were "signs and wonders" produced by the "working of powers," prodigies beyond human ability expressed in Romans 15:19 as "mighty signs and wonders, by the power of the Spirit of God."

GREATER WORKS

Now this gift of the "workings of power" has to be linked with Christ's promise in John 14:12–16—"Most assuredly, I say to you, he who believes in Me, the works that I do he will do also; and greater works than these will he do, because

I go to My Father.... And I will pray the Father, and He will give you another helper."

Jesus promised these greater works, yet so far as we know, the disciples only performed normal healings, and not one of them exceeded Christ's healing ministry. None of them performed a stupendous wonder like the raising of Lazarus four days after his death. What were the "greater works"? To answer that we shall have to make a small detour.

"Greater things" and mighty deeds of power certainly included healings. The healings of Jesus were called "works." However, Paul classes "gifts of healings" separately. The list of gifts was not meant to be a strict separation of different operations, as they overlap, but he clearly had some difference in mind between miraculous healings and "miracles."

Could it be raising the dead? Possibly, as that is not healing. However, it must be something else too, as the Corinthians are not said to have raised the dead, though they came "short in no gift" (1 Cor. 1:7), and many of them had died (1 Cor. 11:30).

It would include creative wonders such as making new eyes or ear drums, or the repair of bones damaged by accident or osteoarthritis. The gifts overlap, and what we might call a healing on one occasion could be classed as a miracle on another. There are some curious occurrences, miraculous in the scientifically impossible sense. Cures take place where there seems to be no physical change but function is inexplicably restored. An eye, perhaps, still appears to be damaged yet has clear vision; hands that appear twisted with arthritis can be flexed and are pain free; people walk who ought not to be able to walk.

For further help, we turn to what Jesus promised about "greater works." He Himself performed the greatest possible cures. Their magnitude was never exceeded by the apostles. Yet it was Christ Himself who spoke of His own disciples exceeding the greatness of His works, doing "greater works." It is quite obvious that it would have to be a different kind of divine wonder beyond what was ever seen in His ministry. Jesus's promise showed that these greater works would be by the Holy Spirit (John 14:12–17).

Now, notice that He repeated the same promise in Acts 1:4–5, 8. On that occasion He spoke of other works, which were not healings. In verse 8 Jesus promised the disciples power, the same word (*dunamis*) used in 1 Corinthians 12. But power for what? It was far more than healing. It was for one special duty, that of world evangelism. "You shall be witnesses to Me…to the end of the earth" (Acts 1:8).

There was another display of divine power, which was never really seen before Christ and which was to be a prophetic sign of the end times—to "turn many to righteousness" (Dan. 12:3). There were no revivals in the Old Testament, as the Holy Spirit was not given. At best only reformations took place by royal command.

That work of world witness called for the comprehensive working of God through His disciples, sufficient to meet every demand and to battle through the entire world in opposition. It was a work that Jesus did not carry out but left to those who follow Him. To bring deliverance to millions, helpless in every bond of sin, and to change the thinking of the entire world are something greater than was seen in the earthly ministry of Christ. Christian conversion is greater than any healing. Salvation is God's greatest work, the perfection of His power.

When Paul first came to Corinth, carrying out the witness task, he said he came "in weakness, in fear, and in much trembling" (1 Cor. 2:3). Some believe that he was suffering from a recurrent infection such as malaria, from a weakness picked up on his travels, or from beatings and hardship. Yet he described his preaching as being "in demonstration of the Spirit and of power" (v. 4). The effect was that a Christian church of blood-washed believers existed amid the spiritual poverty of an idolatrous city.

God's power enabled Paul to carry on despite his bodily weakness. He admitted to a "thorn in the flesh" (2 Cor. 12:7) but triumphed over it by the mighty grace that God had given to him—"strengthened with all might, according to His glorious power, for all patience and longsuffering with joy" (Col. 1:11). He sees himself as an example of the power of God working in him in that way "as dying, and behold we live"—the Lord saying, "My strength [dunamis] is made perfect in weakness" (2 Cor. 6:9; 12:9).

Here is that perfection of power indicated by Jesus as

"greater." Paul calls it "the exceeding greatness of His power" (Eph. 1:19), divine power manifested in the most perfect and superlative sense. He speaks of it being in "earthen vessels," in fragile flesh, those men and women mocked and persecuted by a harsh and cruel age (2 Cor. 4:7). The Corinthians obliged him to boast of the great things and "signs of an apostle" (which Paul said was a foolish thing). He spoke of the power of God sustaining him under the most overwhelming pressures and enabling him to carry the gospel everywhere (2 Cor. 11). "If I must boast, I will boast in the things which concern my infirmity.... For when I am weak, then I am strong" (2 Cor. 11:30; 12:10).

The power in evidence in one man, the apostle Paul, has since been seen on a world scale. The persistence of faith and the amazing endurance of Jesus's followers have come to be accepted as commonplace. Looking at Christian beginnings and then at the subsequent opposition against the unarmed and defenseless followers of Jesus, century after century even to this day, some extraordinary power has to be admitted. We also have the miracle of the church—a compound of every kind of miracle. The "exceeding greatness" of divine power was seen more in the heroic endurance of believers and in the expansion of the church against all resistance than in any physical healing.

Jesus did speak of "he who believes in Me" doing greater works. But there was a greater work done by the whole church. First, it carried the kingdom of God outside the borders of Israel and then to vastly more people worldwide than Christ, in the flesh, ever could address in the small land of Israel. Jesus spoke of His own anointing by the Spirit, which He constantly referred to as the Father's works, but He particularly related it to Isaiah 61:1, to "preach good tidings [the gospel] to the poor." That work is being done on a scale physically impossible to Christ.

For what purpose did the Father send the Holy Spirit? Without any question it was to make it possible to preach the gospel to every creature on earth. Paul describes it as to bring the nations into the obedience of the gospel. The consuming passion and work of Christ was "to seek and to save that which was lost" (Luke 19:10). Jesus was never just a wonder worker. First and foremost He was, and is, a Savior. It was that work that took Him to that Roman cross. That was the ultimate purpose of His earthly life. It was not for some social good—just to feed multitudes—but for the redemption of mankind. That was uppermost in His mind. Any talk of "greater works" has to be in line with His own "great work," to save the lost. Salvation is the greatest labor and the greatest marvel God ever undertook.

Paul spoke far more of the saving power of God than of any physical miracle. He saw the Cross producing the greatest wonders of all, men and women being "made alive, who were dead in trespasses and sins" (Eph. 2:1). "My speech and my preaching were not with persuasive words of human wisdom, but in demonstration of the Spirit of power" (1 Cor. 2:4). For what purpose? "That your faith should not be in the wisdom of men but in the power of God" (v. 5). A miracle healing only confirmed the greater wonder, the gospel. Writing to the Thessalonians, Paul makes this comment: "Our gospel did not come to you in word only, but also in power, and in the Holy Spirit and in much assurance" (1 Thess. 1:5). He then goes on to say "And you became followers of us and of the Lord, having received the word in much affliction, with joy of the Holy Spirit" (v. 6).

We have already remarked on the fact that the mightiest of the inspired prophets all failed to procure anything very much in the way of national repentance. The only success was perhaps that of Jonah in Nineveh, a non-Jewish city. His words frightened them into change of course. But Isaiah was sent to "make the heart of this people dull, and their ears heavy, and shut their eyes" (Isa. 6:10). The only thing that the prophets spoke of was judgment, with only the most distant rays of hope. They were sent to "overturn, overturn." "I have sent to you all My servants the prophets, rising early and sending them.... But they did not listen or incline their ear to turn from their wickedness" (Jer. 44:4–5).

But as soon as Peter, the first preacher of the age of the long-promised outpoured Spirit, opened his lips, the impact was like nobody had ever seen on earth before. Jesus's preaching had no such result. In fact He spoke of Capernaum's lack of repentance despite the miracles He had performed there. But to those who believed on Him, to them He opened up a new prospect of greater things. He gave to Peter the keys of the kingdom. That is, Peter would be the first one to unlock the door of the kingdom by the keys, and those keys were the Word of the Cross and the power of the Spirit. The glorious "opening day" of the age of the Spirit came on the Day of Pentecost. Immediately three thousand came into the kingdom of God, pushing aside the old religious inhibitions.

There are several repetitions, in some form or other, of the Great Commission. (See, for example, Matthew 28:16–20; Mark 16:15–20; Luke 24:48–49; Acts 1:8.) In all of them, the idea of a supernatural power is spoken of, primarily, for the work of evangelism. There was never any thought in the New Testament but of a revival force attending the preaching of the gospel—if the unconverted were present to hear it, of course. The great work of God is salvation—nothing in all the Scriptures exceeds the value placed upon it, and they refer to it constantly. God's salvation is great because He is great.

The words "workings of powers" are plural. This suggests a variety of operations. Evangelism included healings, as we read: "The Lord working with them and confirming the word through the accompanying signs" (Mark 16:20). The work of world redemption called for many gifts, and the gift of miracles included healings, endurance, and the power of God to change the hearts of men and women. Every conversion is a work of power—a miracle of all miracles. The work of Jesus touched some lives, but those He sends reach multiplied masses, and they see miracle after miracle among the most remote and depraved in the world. The lost are found and saved.

THE INEXPLICABLE MIRACLE

Some miracles seem to bring more than one gift into play. For example, let me tell you about Mrs. Heidi Tufte of Norway. I gave a banquet in Oslo, and Mrs. Tufte attended. While I was speaking, the Lord said to me, "Rebuke paralysis." I interrupted what I was saying and told the people that the Holy Spirit was telling me to rebuke paralysis. I did so in a few words and in the name of Jesus.

What I had not seen was that there was a woman at the back of that big hall in a wheelchair—Mrs. Tufte. The moment I had rebuked paralysis, something shot through her system, and she began "churning within her day and night." About a week later she awoke one morning with strange sensations, which quite frightened her; life was flowing through her previously lifeless limbs.

She jumped out of bed and began to cry. Her husband wanted to support her, knowing her paralyzed state, but it was not necessary. "I am healed!" she exclaimed. Overcome with joy, they embraced and dropped down on their knees to give thanks and glory to God.

The news spread across Norway like wildfire, and Mrs. Tufte received flower bouquets from people rejoicing with her from across the land. To this day she leads a normal life, perfectly healed.

Unbelief can be ingenious in its arguments, but this type of miracle disposes of some of the so-called explanations invented to avoid giving glory to God. This healing was not by suggestion from me, since I was not present and had never spoken to her. Nor was it self-suggestion, for she was asleep when the healing life began to course through her body—it woke her up. It disposes of the idea that it was merely a natural recession; in fact, her paralysis was a genetic fault. It was not coincidence—for the healing to occur within a week of my prayer, after a lifetime of illness, is beyond the realms of the wildest coincidence. This was no case of wrong diagnosis or mind over matter.

The gifts operating in such a remarkable cure would be discernment, faith, and miracles, as well as authority, which is another gift not listed by Paul.

There is one other issue relating to the "working of mighty deeds." Here and there comes a suggestion of the Spirit of God as a vast complex of power. "The Spirit of the LORD shall rest upon Him, the Spirit of wisdom and understanding, the Spirit of counsel and of might, the Spirit of knowledge and of the fear of the LORD" (Isa. 11:2). The Holy Spirit is all those Spirits in one Spirit.

Paul uses similar language in 1 Corinthians 12—many operations, one Spirit. Then Revelation 5:6 speaks of "the seven Spirits of God sent out into all the earth"—seven being the number of divine perfection.

We must always keep in mind that the Holy Spirit is

God working on earth in human lives. His manifestations are diverse, because, in the work of salvation, all manner of wonders are needed. Jesus spoke of the Spirit anointing Him with a fivefold task of deliverance (Luke 4:18). In short, there is not a single situation among sinners in which the Spirit of God cannot manifest Himself in some appropriate form. His sufficiency meets His servants at the frontier of every new situation and task.

In Africa, we in the Christ for all Nations team have seen sights that only the greatest power in heaven or earth could produce, perhaps greater than have ever been seen but not so great as will be seen. We have seen acres upon acres of people massed together—Muslim, animist, nominal Christian—touched by the Lord; surrendering to Him by thousands upon thousands; being healed; being baptized in the Spirit; giving up their fetishes, idols, stolen goods, and witchcraft emblems; and becoming vigorous witnesses to Christ. State presidents are converted, and Parliaments echo the cry, "Jesus saves!" The whole thing is a miracle—"the working of miracles," not of one kind, but whatever miracle is needed to meet the crisis of man without God. It's the miracle of souls redeemed by the preaching of the Word.

Compared to such tremendous scenes, what are such wonders as an axe head floating in water, fire from heaven, or walking on the water? God is not a sensationalist. He has one primary concern: people—their welfare and destiny. That interest has to be the measure of all greatness and power.

CHAPTER 13

PROPHECY

P ROPHECY IS TODAY taking a premier place in the charismatic scene beyond any other endowment of the Spirit. Therefore we need to hold it up to the mirror of the Word. We are in good company—prophecy was the gift Paul wanted all to enjoy in Corinth. "Pursue love, and desire spiritual gifts, but especially that you may prophesy....For you can all prophesy one by one" (1 Cor. 14:1, 31).

In this wish he was especially thinking of gifts operating in services of worship. Obviously prophecy, tongues, and interpretation will be for the profit of all mainly when a congregation is in session.

The whole of 1 Corinthians 14 assumes that Paul is thinking of gifts when the people congregate. Some verses state it: for example, "If...an unbeliever or an uninformed person comes in" (v. 24); "Whenever you come together" (v. 26); "in church" (v. 28); "another who sits by" (v. 30); and "in all the churches of the saints" (v. 33). His great thought is the edifying of the church, especially by speech gifts. He throws gifts together in several lists, in no special order, but he always includes the gift of tongues, which, together with interpretation, takes on the character of prophecy.

Again we should note exactly what it says: "The manifestation of the Spirit is given to each one for the profit of all: for to one is given the word of wisdom through the Spirit...to another prophecy" (1 Cor. 12:7–10). We would not distort what Paul meant if we called it "a word of prophecy."

A prophecy is a manifestation, but again we have to be careful to distinguish between prophecy in its varied forms. If we refer to "the gift of prophecy," we ought to know precisely what it means. This Corinthian chapter simply says "to another [is given] prophecy," and the noun is singular. It is a manifestation of the Spirit of prophecy. Now that does not constitute a gift in the outright sense; that is, the ability to prophesy anytime a subject wants—to make prophecies at will. No such power is handed over. It is not a personal presentation to anybody. All the *charismata* are still in the Spirit's control. However, we shall see in what sense there is a gift of prophecy.

We are given this useful information: "The spirits of the prophets are subject to the prophets" (1 Cor. 14:32), but of course we can only prophesy by, and in subjection to, the Holy Spirit. Nevertheless, something is given, and the Greek word *didomi* is used here to show that, in a real sense, it is something given; that is, each utterance. That giving, however, must be understood in the sense of the whole context of 1 Corinthians and not as a complete gift in our common modern sense.

We can put it this way: with all vocal gifts, the will of God and the will of man come together in harmony. While prophecy is not to utter glibly whatever enters our heads anytime we fancy and preface it with "I, the Lord, do say unto thee," it is also true that the Lord encourages the bold prophet who steps out in faith and initiative. The principle here is that the prophet is the servant of the Holy Spirit. The Spirit is not the servant of a prophet, but the Spirit works with the prophet. The Spirit does so because people are tied by time and circumstance.

Paul, in this Scripture passage, makes much of prophecy. He says we should all pray that we may prophesy and adds, "I wish you all spoke with tongues, but even more that you prophesied" (1 Cor. 14:5). The churches of Jesus are prophetic institutions. They exist because of the work of the Holy Spirit, who is "the spirit of the prophets." All church activity should be by the Spirit and in the Spirit. The Spirit of prophecy should characterize every church and its gatherings. That does not mean there must be constant spectacular display but that the prophetic Spirit should charge the hearts of all concerned. The scholar James Dunn puts it starkly— "Without prophecy the community cannot exist as the body of Christ; it has been abandoned by the Lord."[1]

THE FALSE

The subject of prophecy is ancient and vast. It calls for discrimination and judgment. The true and the false are not always easy to discern. That was so long before the Christian age. It was certainly so in apostolic times, and it has been so ever since. A great deal of prophesying has always tended to make it commonplace, and some have always despised it. The people listened to Ezekiel with no better impression than listening to a pleasant song, he complained. Even the apostles showed some hesitations, insisting on proof that they were genuine. "Don't quench the Spirit, don't despise prophecies, but prove all things, hold fast the good, from every form of evil abstain" (1 Thess. 5:19–21, literal translation).

It is a tremendous claim to say one speaks in the name of the Lord. We should not believe it just because somebody claims it. We should check the credentials of all who profess to be prophets and, even then, check their prophecies. Uncritical hearing is disapproved of in Scripture. Jesus said, "Take heed how you hear" (Luke 8:18).

Human nature approves what it likes to hear—"smooth sayings," as in the last days of the Judean kings, whose household prophets always gave optimistic (but wrong) predictions. Christian bodies have sometimes accepted prophecies simply because they confirmed their theological or organizational dogmas, and thus prophecies are prejudged rather than judged. An honest search of Scripture is the only way. We must not ignore this simple rule: "By the mouth of two or three witnesses every word may be established" (Matt. 18:16). Prophecy has been misused to stifle dissident opinion, as when Jeremiah was put in a pit for disagreeing with the rest of the so-called prophets. We cannot test prophecy by ballot, or majority opinion. *Vox populi* (the voice of the people) is rarely *vox Dei* (the voice of God).

The long history of disaster exemplifies and confirms warnings by Christ and the apostles to treat prophetic utterances with caution. We must always check them against the Word of God. We are always responsible for what we do, even if we are obeying somebody else's prophecy. Eve found that being deceived did not make wrong right. The results of false prophesyings boomerang on the deceiver.

Prophesiers moved around the early churches. Many believers were illiterate, the churches were young, and there was little Christian writing or experience to guide them. Teaching was needed, and prophets were therefore welcomed. They arrived announcing their own inspiration, and it is not surprising that they were given great credence. For those scattered groups of early believers needing teaching, beggars could not be choosers.

All the apostolic leaders faced this problem. John, for example, laid down one test—unless prophets taught that Christ had come in the flesh, they were not to be entertained or given hospitality. This particular rule was needed locally because the idea was becoming prevalent that God could never submit to crucifixion and that it was only a phantom Christ that could be crucified, never God. He only seemed to be real (called *docetism*).

That was one error drifting in on the prevailing religious winds. There are signs that this teaching affected the Corinthians, whose claims to be "spiritual" meant that they were familiar with deeper levels of life. They believed that now even their flesh was different and that they had already passed through resurrection. Paul met this dangerous nonsense in chapter 15 by speaking of the resurrection of the body. Teachings like this, spread by prophetic claims, gave apostolic leaders much anxiety.

Even in Moses's time tests had to be laid down (Deut. 13), and Jeremiah also challenged false prophets. It is true that Israel's prophets were unique, but all the nations had "prophets," or those considered inspired, especially the oracles, such as those at Delphos, Dodona, Delosi, and the guardians of the Sibylline Books. In the temples of this or that god, there were women sitting on tripods to give forth their oracles who often jabbered in an occult trance or ecstasy. Priests claimed to be able to interpret the usually ambiguous prophecies.[2]

There is an instance of this in 1 Kings 22:15. Micaiah was asked by the king to prophesy about the proposal to attack Syria. At first he gave the king what the king wanted to hear, but it was ambiguous: "Go and prosper, for the LORD will deliver it into the hand of the king!" King Ahab thought it would fall into his hands, but in fact it fell into the hand of the king of Syria.

Prophets were common enough. The schools of the prophets were a vital element in Israel, and, no doubt, we owe much that was preserved and written down as Scripture to them. But after the Babylonian exile, the role of prophet became less evident and even suspect. Prophets "speaking comfortable things" had let Israel down, and absolute national catastrophe was the result. Nobody was anxious to "wear a robe of coarse hair to deceive," as Zechariah said, after the Jewish exile (Zech. 13:4). They were "ashamed" to assume the prophetic mantle. John the Baptist's call was so real that he did wear typical prophetic garb.

Abuse of spiritual gifts has been a major calamity in the church. If what we read about the Montanists of the second century is true (though we only have writings from their enemies), they made irresponsible, extravagant claims of the Holy Spirit speaking and false predictions of the kingdom of God being set up in Phrygia. This led to a tradition in the church that frowned on spiritual manifestations and excitement. It was considered fanatical "enthusiasm." This was perhaps one of the saddest and most damaging church decisions of all time. The bishops, of course, feared that if the Spirit spoke through lay men and women, their authority could be undermined, and the possible excesses of the Montanists gave them the excuse they needed to suppress what was going on.

History parades before us a heartbreaking series of

pseudo-prophets, or even demon-inspired teachings, that have damaged the church beyond all telling. It would be impossible to think of anything that needs to be treated with greater caution. False prophecy has filled the world with error and unorthodox sects and has even created world religions. Strong as is the prophetic fashion in the church at present, to build on it without constantly checking by the plumb line of the Word of God would leave an unstable edifice. A church led by prophets will sooner or later be misled. The maxim is, "Should not a people seek their God?" The answer is yes, but... "To the law and to the testimony! If they do not speak according to this word, it is because there is no light in them" (Isa. 8:19–20).

"When they say to you, 'Seek those who are mediums and wizards, who whisper and mutter,' should not a people seek their God?" (v. 19). People seek the dead on behalf of the living—why should they not consult God? The long history of imposters, charlatans, occultists, cult leaders, and false and self-deceived ecstatics does not mean there is no true divine inspiration. On the contrary, it proves there must be the real; counterfeit coins can only copy the genuine. The devil would not neglect such a strategy. He made it his work, even from the beginning in Eden, to offer a counterfeit prophecy, leaving the pair uncertain of the voice of God. He will deploy his own inspired agents to unsettle those who hear the Word of God. These are the birds that devour the seed of the sower (Matt. 13:4).

THE REAL

The Bible cuts a path through the tangle of prophetic claims and shows us the real. The whole Bible is a prophecy. It moves onward to a climax.

The Old Testament consists of three sections: the Law, the Prophets, and the Writings. The Prophets included historical books. They are part of the unfolding revelation of the ultimate aims of God. God's intentions began to be indicated way back in Genesis 1:27–28: "God created man…male and female He created them….Then God blessed them." In Genesis 3:15 God said to the serpent who deceived Eve, "I will put enmity between you and the woman, and between your seed and her Seed; He shall bruise your head, and you shall bruise His heel." This looked far ahead to Christ and to His final triumph.

The call of Abraham pointed to far-off divine plans to bless all the families of the earth. Abraham "saw" Christ's day, and looked beyond to the eternal city of God (Gen. 12:1–3; John 8:56; Heb. 11:10). All prophecy, including the gift of prophecy, should move in that same all-important direction to focus the hopes, faith, and conduct of us all toward the realization of eternal redemption and the kingdom.

We need to be aware that prophecies may be trivial, even if they are delivered in resounding and dramatic tones. They can be side issues, unrelated to the wider interests of the kingdom and to what God is contemplating. Prophecy not born from the womb of the redemption plan of God is worthless. It is in the value category of palmistry and the horoscope. Somebody has said, "If a prophecy is not of God, it is too slight to be proved, and if it is of God, it ought not to be proved." That is flawed logic. We need to know whether it is of God—that is what testing is about.

Prophecy is a manifestation of the presence of God and therefore places hearers before God. It challenges our direction and brings pressure upon us to move only in accordance with His movings.

One of the finest descriptions of the true prophet actually comes from that alien and strange character Balaam in Numbers 24:4. He says he is one who "hears the words of God, who sees the vision of the Almighty, who falls down, with eyes wide open." "The vision of the Almighty" refers to God's vision for mankind, and Balaam found he could say nothing except in line with God's future for Israel.

The great prophetic book of the New Testament is Revelation. It gives a unique panorama of the grand divine scheme, drawing together elements from all the previous prophecies. It begins, "The Revelation of Jesus Christ, which God gave Him to show His servants—things which must shortly take place" (Rev. 1:1). If the spirit of any prophecy cuts across the general scheme of biblical revelation and the purposes of God in the gospel, and does not relate to these in any sense, then little weight should be attached to it. Either it is devilish or, more likely, human imagination.

PROVE ALL THINGS

A prophet whose words come to pass might be more dangerous than one whose word does not come to pass. The test of a true prophet is not that his words come to pass. Satanic forces can organize that also. Deuteronomy 13:1–3, 5 warns us:

> If there arises among you a prophet or a dreamer of dreams, and he gives you a sign or a wonder, and the sign or the wonder comes to pass, of which he spoke to you, saying, "Let us go after other gods"—which you have not known—"and let us serve them," you shall not listen to the words of that prophet or dreamer of dreams…[he] shall be put to death.

The evidence that a prophecy is not true becomes apparent, of course, when it fails to come to pass.

> If you say in your heart, "How shall we know the word which the Lord has not spoken?"—when a prophet speaks in the name of the Lord, if the thing does not happen or come to pass, that is the thing which the Lord has not spoken; the prophet has spoken it presumptuously; you shall not be afraid of him.
> —Deuteronomy 18:21–22

A true man of God can nevertheless speak from his own mind and be mistaken. There is a difference between a false prophet and one who speaks presumptuously. A false prophet brings false teaching. A failed prophecy merely shows a man is speaking out of himself. Nathan spoke out of his own mind when he told David that he should go ahead and build the temple. Later he had to correct this mistake, and he brought God's own mind, not to build, to David. Isaiah told Hezekiah that he would die, but he had to return almost at once with a different message that he would live. In several places Paul heard prophecies that he did not accept, and they were not infallible.

There is such a thing as prophesying according to the proportion of our faith. When God spoke to me to build the world's largest gospel tent to seat thirty-four thousand people, I met with the brethren of my board to discuss it. After we had gone into the matter, we prayed together, and one of the men present began to prophesy. He began, "Thus saith the Lord: Thousands shall be saved under this roof." Then he stopped and said to us, "Excuse me, this is not what the Holy Spirit said, but I did not have the faith to utter it. Let me start again. Thus says the Lord: Millions will be saved under this roof." How right he was, but it was not just under the canvas roof. The tent would have to be filled for many years to house enough unconverted people to amount to millions of conversions. But a work was beginning under that roof that would continue under the canopy of the glory of God as we moved across the African continent, in which we actually witnessed those millions of precious people being saved.

There are prophets who abrogate to themselves special authority in order to impose their ideas upon others; they even believe that their own interpretation of Scripture is given by revelation and is not to be challenged. One teacher asserted, "God has told me what such-and-such a scripture means," though it was obviously a distorted interpretation. If we are to prove all things, we cannot let such claims to authority go unchallenged. Of all people, the prophet must submit to the judgment of others. A prophet's own claim that he speaks by the word of the Lord is not enough. God has left authority with the churches. Jesus told us to beware of such dogmatists.

Anyone bringing a word from the Lord should realize what that means—that it is an implicit claim to be a prophet according to Scripture. They ought to be really sure that God has spoken before they speak. A person claiming to be a prophet, who is nothing of the kind, is an abomination in the sight of God.

MECHANICS OF PROPHECY

Some prophecy is in the first person—"I, the Lord, do say unto thee..." This is an awesome claim. Sometimes it is proved not to be the Lord God speaking but only Jack or Mary. A man may claim he is "standing in the counsel of the Lord." Let it be recognized that this is an exclusive distinction above other believers, for we all have the Word of God, which is the counsel of the Lord and in which we stand. Notwithstanding the gifts of wisdom, knowledge, and prophecy, Paul could say to the Corinthians, "He who is spiritual judges all things, yet he himself is rightly judged by no one. For 'who has known the mind of the LORD that he may instruct Him?' But we have the mind of Christ" (1 Cor. 2:15–16). It is therefore hardly legitimate for one man to place himself on a higher level than all believers who "have the mind of Christ."

There is the question of language in prophecy. Often the English lapse into the three-hundred-year-old form of their tongue found in the Authorized or King James Version of the Bible. Actually it was becoming dated even when that Bible first appeared. It is a tradition, copied from one to another through the decades, especially by people who were deeply versed in the King James Version. However, it should not detract from the value of what is said. The reason prophecy is often couched in this style is because it is filtered through our minds—which, as far as religion is concerned, has come to us from the Word of God in Elizabethan form. It is a religious habit of speech often heard in prayer, as in the Anglican Common Book of Prayer. It is the picture, not the frame, that matters.

We can use everyday speech, which certainly was always the case in Bible days. To dress up uninspired spiritual clichés in a majestic literary style, hoping to sound like Isaiah in full flight, and prefaced by "I the Lord do say unto thee" is wrong. If our word is from the Holy Spirit, we need not try to make it appear so.

THE OLD TESTAMENT PROPHET AND
THE NEW TESTAMENT PROPHET

The designation "prophet" covers all manner of inspired speakers, even the false. The Old Testament prophet is not the same as the New Testament prophet. In fact, Christ said the prophets prophesied until John the Baptist, indicating that was the end of an era. Some differences can be mentioned.

The pre-Christian prophet was God's mouthpiece to those who had no direct contact with the Lord. What the Lord had to say was revealed to the prophets and through them to Israel and to some outside Israel. Individuals, as well as the nation, had access to the will of God through the prophet or through the high priest if he had the Urim and Thummim. Even the Edomites could have had that access (Isa. 21:12).

The Hebrew prophets were lone figures—the Pentecostal or charismatic who prophesies is not, but he is part of the prophetic group, the church. All believers know the Lord and do not need anybody to stand between them and God. They are God's new covenant people in a new relationship and know the Lord (Heb. 8). No one needs to inquire of the Lord on another's behalf.

We have said elsewhere that there is no conception of higher or lower but of one body with many parts. Some may be leaders, which gives them prominence but not superiority. Those they lead are playing their own roles and are therefore not inferiors but equals in God's sight. "Office" is read into passages in the New Testament relating to elders and deacons, but no such word or intent is there. The thought is always function not position. "Be submissive to one another, and be clothed with humility" (1 Pet. 5:5). This applies to the prophet as well as anybody else. There is no office of prophet to which a believer can be officially appointed. Prophets are not judged on whether they are commissioned by men or not.

There is no place for an intermediary between men and the Holy Spirit when all are energized and gifted by the Spirit as "a royal priesthood" (1 Pet. 2:9). "Call no man Master," Jesus said. "Be shepherds, not lording over those entrusted to you." (See Matthew 23:9–12.) There is no hierarchy, for all are servants of all, and in Christ there is neither male nor female. The laity does not depend on an elite authority, for all have charismatic or apostolic powers. The pastor who does not delegate will see the limbs of the body deteriorate. A denominational leader once demanded that only evangelists with experience should evangelize. But how can a man get experience unless he evangelizes?

Believers under the new covenant are not to be directed in their lives through any third party. "For as many as are led by the Spirit of God, these are sons of God" (Rom. 8:14). That is our royal privilege and freedom. To assert the right of delegated authority and to delegate authority over to others is contrary to the kingdom principle and is precisely in step with the present secular world system. Jesus never directed people's decisions, even those of His own disciples. He gives us freedom, and whatever advice we take or whomever we obey, we are responsible for what we do, prophecy or not.

The prophets of Israel often spoke to the whole nation. The New Testament prophet does not. Actually the Hebrew prophets, before Christ, spoke to the nation as God's people, and the Christian prophet speaks to the church as God's people. No New Testament figure after John the Baptist went as Jeremiah or Amos did with a commission to address national affairs. In the time of the kings of Israel some prophets, such as Nathan, were retained in some kind of official capacity for this purpose of national guidance. Samuel and the charismatic judges acted as national leaders, but there is nothing like this in the Christian dispensation.

The voice of God to the nations today comes through the whole body of the church. What Isaiah was to Israel, the whole church is to Germany, Britain, or America. The church's existence, way of life, and principles of service should be a constant challenge to the ways of nations. There were times when it was said, "There was no vision in the land." When the church ceases to bring God's vision to a nation, calamity is near, which is why the church must be charismatic. All who led early Israel were charismatic, until Solomon. The weakness of Israel subsequently was that they had a Davidic dynasty but not a Davidic charismatic anointing.

The prophets in the apostolic church did not have a fixed office, nor did the apostles, teachers, evangelists, or pastors.

God gave people of that type to the church whether they were given recognition or not. Men may appoint, but only God can endow, and God gives little heed to our arbitrary choices or elections. What any church should do is set out in Acts 13, namely to separate men to the work to which God has called them. Jealousy that God has called or gifted an individual has so often frustrated that call. Those in leadership have sometimes closed the doors of opportunity to God's own chosen, just as Saul opposed David. If a prophet may not be appointed, he should at least be recognized.

A prophet should also be known. That is implicit in 1 Corinthians. For a stranger to invade worship, addressing everybody uninvited, is not merely discourteous but out of order. There are those who prophesy by post, in printed circulars, or in magazines whose names are unfamiliar to us. Prophecies come from organizations—can an organization prophesy? Unless readers of these effusions know who the prophets are and what their credentials are, they can be disregarded. Isaiah we know, Paul we know, but who are they?

HOW DOES PROPHETIC UTTERANCE COME?

The first essential is the sense of the Spirit drawing or leading us in that direction. The sense of the prophetic spirit moving us may come even before we know what the burden of the Lord is. The prophets were called to speak and then given the message later (Isa. 6; Jer. 1). One cannot speak from a cold heart. Someone speaking with tongues may bring to us an instant leading to interpret. Some prophesiers need that stimulus and never otherwise speak. In that case their gift is interpretation. The word of God may come to us as a gradual growing of a burden from the Lord or as a flash of brilliant illumination. It can be in the mind as words, a thought, a significant picture, a vision, a dream, or an inner conviction or impulse, but it will be expressed in words. Sometimes it will seem that the process is instantaneous, the thought and the words flowing together, extemporaneously, as if from outside oneself.

We cannot "work up" the voice of God within us, nor can we think it up. It comes from heaven. That is true, but how we give it, and when, is entirely our own responsibility. It can be written down and read to those whom God shows us. Isaiah and Jeremiah were writing prophets. It might be far better expressed with that kind of care. We even read of Elijah sending a prophecy by letter.

The leader of a church or service is there to keep a decent orderliness and also to ensure that no wrong teaching is given. To throw open a meeting to all and sundry is almost a tradition in many assemblies, and the risks it carries are only too well known. Some leaders fail to recognize their responsibility, and they let anything go. Certain situations call for rectification by the graciousness of the Lord. In the case of prophecies, at least, this is scriptural. In larger churches it becomes necessary to check beforehand prophecies that may be given, or at least the prophesiers. This avoids the proceedings becoming a confusing affair. It is commended practice today that prophecies are submitted to the pastor to "prove all things; hold fast that which is good" (1 Thess. 5:21, KJV). Then they can be given at an appropriate part of the worship and, if necessary, made audible by use of sound equipment. Otherwise what is spontaneous can become disorderly.

Speaking with tongues is characteristically spontaneous, however. Paul realized this and offered guidelines for tongues as well as for prophecy. He put it that one speaker should speak only twice or three times at the most. He knew how some would dominate the worship. We are to excel in the manifestation of the Spirit and use wisdom in all things. Some pastors insist that permission to speak with tongues must be given. This avoids anything that is out of keeping with what is going on, but it does create a big risk that the spirit of the prophets is dampened down altogether. To "quench not the Spirit" often calls for a lot of wisdom and loving tact (1 Thess. 5:19).

PROPHETS AND PROPHESIERS

It will help students of the gifts if we say that we must differentiate between prophets and those who prophesy. Our lack of language in the realm of such things makes that easier said than done. There are no criteria in the New Testament to help us discriminate between prophets and those who prophesy.

Presumably those who frequently prophesy may be called prophets, but we are short of words to make rigid distinctions. Paul calls all prophesiers "prophets" in 1 Corinthians 14:29, 32, but even in his thinking a difference seems to exist. He seems to place in different categories those who often prophesy and those who have the normal "signs following" spoken of by Joel ("your sons and your daughters shall prophesy"—Joel 2:28), for Paul asks "Are all prophets?" (1 Cor. 12:29). In Acts 21:9 we read that Philip had four daughters who prophesied— it shuns calling them prophetesses, though this may reflect the age when women were not as free as today.

Not only prophesiers but also tongues-speakers, those healing and working miracles, and others with gift ministries are not given a distinctive name. Prophecy by someone who is regularly heard or by someone only occasionally is the same and equally valuable. A healing by the laying on of hands of an elder does not mean that he has the gift of the gifts of healings, but it is as much a sign of God's love as a healing by the mightiest healer in the world.

God does not distribute titles and medals. Nobody does anything except by the Holy Spirit. What glory can there be to a man? I have as much to do with healings taking place in my crusades as an electric kettle has to do with a nuclear generator. The church has every characteristic since it has the Holy Spirit, but each member has his or her own gift. It is all an organic and charismatic work, but God distributes "to each one individually as He wills" (1 Cor. 12:11).

CHAPTER 14

DISCERNMENT

THE GIFT OF discernment, or more accurately "of discernings of spirits," is not a natural knowledge of people's psychology, much less the power to "see through" everybody and to make the sensational discovery that all human beings are imperfect. Let us note exactly what 1 Corinthians 12:10 says: "to another discerning of spirits." The Greek word for discerning is *diakrisis* and comes from the verb *krino*, which means "to judge."

The discerning of spirits is not a gift to see what is invisible—a demon, for example—but the power to judge what is seen, whether good or bad. "But solid food belongs to those who are of full age, that is, those who by reason of use have their senses exercised to discern [*diakrisis*] both good and evil" (Heb. 5:14).

The Greek *diakrisis* has a meaning of a distinguishing or discerning clearly; a faculty of discerning. To discern means to perceive the difference between. The overall thought is that of "separating" one thing from another. *Diakrisis* is used three times in the New Testament: Romans 14:1; 1 Corinthians 12:10; and Hebrews 5:14.

From this it is clear that the main meaning is not seeing demons but judging what is visible and audible. The gift is not sight but discrimination. It is true that the experience of "seeing" or sensing demons that may be concealing their presence (as they usually do) is not uncommon among Christian believers, and in a general sense this gift may include such discernment, though not necessarily. One can have experiences for which no gift is listed.

Next we should note that the word is plural, "discernings." That is, it is not a general gift of discrimination, but it comes as repeated manifestations as God grants them, as with all gifts or revelations of the Holy Spirit as and when needed. While the Spirit may use anybody anytime, these judgments are often specially given to one individual—we then say they have the gift.

In fact, we are told that others must exercise discrimination about prophecies (1 Cor. 14:29). This does not always need the gift of discernment, though without this gift we could make a mistake and condemn what should be welcomed. The gift is not merely to recognize what is spiritually evil but also what is good. The Spirit of the Lord rested on David, but his brethren did not want to know. The blessed of the Lord are not always an immediate hit with their friends or colleagues!

There are rules by which everybody can judge prophecy and other matters. Usually no supernatural help is needed to "discern" when a person has a demon—it is obvious. The Spirit of all gifts is in the church, and there His manifestations of one kind or another are part of the ongoing ministry of the church, such as healing, tongues, and faith. Particular individuals have a marked ministry in some aspect of the Spirit and so are said to have a gift. Discernment, or more correctly, the power to distinguish clearly between spirits, has to be very evident throughout the body of the church.

The word Paul uses means to differentiate between spirits. The same thing is in 1 John 4:1–3, though a different word is used (*dokimazo*: to prove, to test): "Beloved, do not believe every spirit, but test the spirits, whether they are of God" (1 John 4:1). John continues, "Every spirit that confesses that Jesus Christ has come in the flesh is of God" (v. 2). That is his simple test for one form of false teaching. I know that it sounds as if there may be many spirits that are of God, but John is not saying that. What he is saying is that when spirits seem to be saying that Christ came in the flesh, it is the (one) Spirit of God speaking: "By this you know the Spirit of God" (v. 2). The word *spirit* is used in a broad sense of spiritual manifestations. Actually, in this case, John mainly had in mind an error that was creeping in—later known as Gnosticism—which said the body of Christ on the cross was only a phantom. John does not mention any gift for discerning spirits, but he gives a simple test that anybody can apply. He does, however, insist in connection with this: "But you have an anointing from the Holy One, and you know all things" (1 John 2:20), which does indicate a supernatural discernment.

The gift of discernment overlaps with a word of wisdom, but it especially concerns spirits. We are told in many places to evaluate what is said or done. Believers are not to swallow everything they hear, especially things that purport to be from the Lord or are declared to be God speaking. Uncritical acceptance of so-called prophecies and claims to knowledge and revelation without a proper check is regarded as foolish in Scripture, but unfortunately it is common. It is astonishing how naïve many are. Constantly we see people being deceived, perhaps in marginal matters but often in real error and with fearful results, producing countless new fabricated cults and fanaticism leading even to tragedy and deaths.

In the field of the supernatural gifts this one is vital. There are counterfeits being passed as true currency—hence the remark about "doctrines of demons"—as well as human imitations, calling for the gifts to be subject to judgment. It is the burglar alarm for intruders in the realm of the supernatural gifts. Some have seen a certain logical sequence in the Corinthian list. Certainly putting discernment first seems wise.

The gift of discernment covers the widest field of spiritual interests, not just one small item of discernment of the devil. It is certainly needed in everything, such as in prophecy and other teaching about which we are so often warned in Scripture. Demons do 99 percent of their work unseen without "manifesting," and we have to be sensitive to the "doctrines of demons," which come as new revelation.

The voice of the Spirit is often very quiet. The agitation of our own passions and motives can drown it. Jesus's temptations in the wilderness were remarkable because, in each one, He was tempted to do what seemed to be good for mankind, even backed up by Scripture, but He saw the subtlety of Satan each time. It is more important to judge new teachings than to look for demons in everybody.

PERCEIVING DEMONS

There are various ways this gift has been understood. Dr. Ralph Martin refers to it as the power to judge prophecies and demonic substitutes. D. G. Dunn is a scholar who thinks it is a form of prophecy used as a check against the abuses of other gifts, not merely to judge prophecies as commanded in 1 Thessalonians 5:20–21. It has been seen as "the Spirit-given ability to distinguish the Spirit of God from a demon spirit under whose direction the charismatic exercises a particular gift."[1]

Another writer regards it as a gift to free pastoral life from influences that do not come from God to build up the church. It is doctrinal discernment, making correct, subjective judgments, perhaps of a gift operating in the whole community.

All of these suggestions may well be part of the answer, as Paul only names this gift and does not explain it. One thing it certainly is, namely, is protection against what is spiritually false.

The gift of discernment has been related to the three tests of charismatic happenings in 1 Corinthians 12–14:

- That tongues and prophecies never say Jesus is accursed (1 Cor. 12:3)

- That they are marked by love (1 Cor. 13:4–7)

- That they build up the church (1 Cor. 14:12)

These Bible principles of judgment are not supernatural tests obviously, but the gift of discernment is supernatural and needs to be. There are so many ideas, voices, and teachings entering our minds or even thrown up by our own thoughts that need the discerning eye of God Himself to distinguish good from bad. Our own heart can mislead us, for it is "deceitful above all things" says Jeremiah 17:9. There are signs and wonders, prophecies, and much more phenomena that could "deceive, if possible, even the elect" as Jesus warned us (Mark 13:22).

The gift of discernment can save us from deception, though the Word of God also has that work to do, as a "discerner of the thoughts and intents of the heart" (Heb. 4:12). Many deceptions are successful because believers understand so little of the Word of God. Our own will, the deviousness of our hearts, and the trickery of the enemy—all need to be exposed. The Spirit of God can make us sensitive to the approach of what is or is not of God. "My sheep hear my voice" (John 10:27). There is such a thing as failing to discern what is holy, as some do not "[discern] the Lord's body" (1 Cor. 11:29).

We never read in the New Testament of anyone discerning demons in people's lives. That does not invalidate such experiences, however. From the beginning Peter perceived that Ananias and Sapphira were liars. Then Simon Magus, a sorcerer practicing magic and the black arts, wanted to buy the power of God, and Peter said, "I see that you are poisoned by bitterness and bound by iniquity" (Acts 8:23). The apostle said nothing about demons. To put Simon right, Peter cast no demon out of him but simply told him to repent of his wickedness, and ask God to forgive him. Simon asked Peter to pray for him. These instances may be classed as discernment, prophecy, or a word of knowledge. Everything that the Holy Spirit does cannot possibly be categorized under nine gifts.

Because of the mention of this gift, some go looking for demons to cast out. It has been argued that we must take the initiative in aggression, find the demons, and attack them. Paul certainly did nothing like that. He cast out a demon of divination from a fortune-teller slave girl (Acts 16:18). It needed no discernment, as demon possession rarely does. Everybody in the city knew that she had a spirit, and for days

Paul refused to go on the attack against the power of darkness. However, she pestered him so much that he felt people might associate her and her spirit of divination with the gospel and assume that it was one of Paul's teachings. What he did discern was that she was doing his work no good. The same thing happened with Jesus, for unclean spirits knew Him and said who He was, but Jesus commanded them to be silent. He wanted no recommendation from them. He wanted nobody to be misled into thinking that demons were His friends or went along with him. He cast them out. They were trying to "jump on the bandwagon," as if He had come from some general world of spirit.

The Lord Himself, the disciples, and Philip all cast out demons, but people came to them or were brought to them for that purpose, obviously because they knew that they were possessed. The presence of a demon is usually too appalling to miss, although the devil does not always make himself conspicuous—on the contrary, occult and physical activities advertise his presence too much and inconveniently. He prefers to walk in the dark or to masquerade as an angel of light. In fact those who have tried to be possessed or to "have" a spirit or a spirit guide do not always find it that easy. Normally the powers of darkness prefer to work undercover. Even those with a familiar spirit or spirit guide do not rave like the Gadarene madman, out of whom Jesus cast a legion of spirits, which were tearing him in every direction. Nevertheless, unclean presences often cling to those who try to deal with these dark spirits and who try to contact the dead.

The gift of discernment is given for other deceptions as well. There are many teachings today that have a sound of the truth and seem good, but they are not the gospel; for example, the popular teaching that we are potential saints, children of God, and only need to realize it to live above ourselves—the power of positive thinking. It all looks so right and plausible. It certainly is a bad thing to have a deep sense of inferiority, but confession of sin and true salvation are a glorious and effective remedy, giving the heart knowledge that one is a son of God. There is no shortcut. We must repent at the foot of the cross in lowliness of heart before we can rise in new life. Discernment will differentiate between the seemingly good and the real.

OCCULT DISTRACTION

It is hard to know why the occult receives such major attention from Christian people. In some areas, of course, as I find in Africa especially, demons are a daily reality, and I find myself on a major battleground. Usually the enemy works on a far broader front than that, however, not merely in the one sector of physical manifestations. We should learn from Paul, as we pointed out just now. He did nothing about a possessed person until the situation demanded it. Demon hunting is something for which there is notably no apostolic example. However, it fascinates some, to the exclusion of tackling the common evils of depravity and unbelief in the human heart or preaching the Gospel, the Word of God, which is the sword of the Spirit and the only offensive weapon Paul mentions in our armory in Ephesians 6.

Smith Wigglesworth always preached about faith in God, but there are "experts" now teaching nothing but about demons. There are even schools who train in the lore of demonology instead of the whole counsel of God. They justify their schools on the suspicious grounds that the Bible says little about casting out evil spirits, and they have to redress the shortcomings of Scripture and teach from experience. However, 2 Peter 1:3–4 says the "great and precious promises" are "all things that pertain to life and godliness."

Some extremely dangerous practices can emerge here. Many like to put on their boxing gloves and, with a fierce and menacing air, stand face-to-face with Satan, with violence and shouting and commanding, perhaps for hours. One demonologist told a twenty-four-year-old graduate that she needed the demon to be beaten out of her—to which humiliation she submitted hopefully but without feeling any improvement. This should never be—it is unhealthy, unedifying, and unbiblical. Some violent exorcisms have caused death and even criminal prosecution. The press reported a case in London and another in Australia. The word of command should be all that is needed in most cases, as we see in the New Testament instances of deliverances. The devil meanwhile gets on with his real job of deceiving the nations, not merely haunting houses or other physical activities.

The work of God most certainly includes the casting out of demons. In our gospel crusades in Africa, we find ourselves in areas in which the very atmosphere is polluted with demons. Witchcraft abounds. Recently some demon-possessed men cast spells and danced around my hotel all night. When I have begun to preach and to mention the name of Jesus, often scores of demons manifest themselves immediately, and victims begin to writhe, scream, and disturb the proclamation of the Word. I do not stop preaching, for that is the strategy of the devil. For the few or so manifesting demon possession, multitudes want to hear the gospel. We have trained workers ready to lead the devil-possessed away and to deal with them away from the crowd, while the message of the gospel goes forward. We are not there to put on demonstrations but to preach the gospel.

Some claim to have the gift of discernment but use complicated tests and multipage questionnaires, not to mention fearful suggestions upon open-minded people. To investigate Spirit-filled believers for such dark powers is surely a reflection upon the salvation promises of God. The Holy Spirit makes our bodies His temples, and He would never come to an agreement with a devil to share such a small apartment or tolerate such a foul and illegal squatter. If our lives are hidden with Christ in God, and we have a demon, then it would mean that the demon hidden in us is also hidden in God! That is unthinkable.

If believers have anything clinging to them, it is the old life, the old man. In that case Scripture makes us responsible to "put off the old man with his deeds" and to "put on Christ" (Col. 3:9; Gal. 3:27). No Christian was ever exorcised in Bible times. They were guilty of many sins and weaknesses, but it is never put down to the indwelling of an unclean spirit. The answer to faults was not exorcism but exercise in godliness, casting off (not out) the unfruitful works of darkness.

Much is made of Christ's words to Peter, "Get behind me, Satan," but this was no exorcism, and there was no sign of a demon manifesting or leaving him. After all, Jesus had just said that Peter was "blessed," and God had revealed the identity of Jesus to him. Peter could not be blessed of God and have a demon at the same time, but he could say something very human, which thrust itself into the heart of Jesus like a dagger of the old temptation in the wilderness.

JUDGING THE SPIRITS

Where then should we be alert for demon powers? The major area of satanic danger to the church is given as "doctrines of demons" (1 Tim. 4:1); that is, teachings and innovations thrown into the ring by the enemy. They come from all quarters, religious and secular. Some are subtle half untruths buried in seemingly spiritual or pious expressions. Some may be scriptures, in fact, such as those Satan tried out on Jesus in the wilderness. Claims of new revelations have been made, which they say not even the apostles understood! Scripture speaks of false teachers, false prophets, false christs, false pastors, false brethren, false guides, lying wonders, and wolves in sheep's clothing not only from outside in the world but also rising up among believers "speaking perverse things" (Acts 20:30).

Satan is behind the divisions—the church offshoots, little companies around some leader emphasizing some pet dogma of his own, people majoring on minor matters, groups with issues blown up like balloons by windbag leaders, or petty complaints given a disproportionate importance. Satan's arrows are errors, opening a running wound in the side of the body of Christ, bleeding away the testimony, as the devil planned and also as God forewarned us in the Word. Without the gift of the discerning of spirits, the church is weakened and divided everywhere.

Even outside the church there are major deceptions, which, unless watched, will creep into the church itself—and indeed have done so. The enemy's job is to provide intellectual interest for those who do not know the truth, who pretend to search for it but reject the truth of the gospel. The twentieth century was marked by the end of one of the greatest anti-God movements, Marxist communism, which made war on the church for three quarters of a century before being recognized as the empty evil it was. God's people everywhere knew it was sinister, but they were derided as "right wing."

Even now, no doubt this hydra-headed and anti-God political monster will struggle yet to survive—as does Nazism.

Western thinking has also been dominated by secular and godless theories. Satan has planted agents in the highest educational establishments and even in theological seminaries. Non-Christian or anti-Christian concepts have destroyed the spiritual backbone of nation after nation, beginning with my own country, Germany, where the Bible-doubting cult of intellectualism was hatched during the eighteenth century with the so-called Enlightenment, which spawned the evils of revolution and war.

Everywhere the effects have been frightening. The biblical grounds of morality are being destroyed. Without any inner light each decade ever since has brought a worse wave of heathenism, evil for evil's sake, destruction, and even murder for the sheer pleasure of it, both by governments and devil-inspired individuals. People look for will-o'-the-wisp "new political initiatives" because they cannot discern that behind so much of the upheaval in the world is the "prince of the power of the air, the spirit who now works in the sons of disobedience" (Eph. 2:2). The origins of all behavior are moral and spiritual. The believer has a means by which to shun these vastly popular but corrupting fashions—the gift of the discerning of spirits.

For the apostles, the world was full of pagan thought. Paul talked about "the wisdom of this world," thinking particularly of the Greek philosophers who never found God and after six centuries of acute intellectual activity were still pagans worshiping at an altar inscribed to "the unknown god." That false wisdom was held in such high worldly esteem, as it is now, that it was infiltrating and warping Christian teaching. Some tried to merge their mystic or philosophic religious ideas with Christianity. Paul could quote them, but he insisted that they were mutually antagonistic.

In fact, the history of church doctrine has largely been the history of attempts to marry the Christian faith with human secular philosophy—everything from Plato to Berkeley and every other fancy and fashion of thought. The gospel has been constantly hacked, chiseled, and molded to fit any and every idea that the devil ever put in human heads. From thousands of churches certainty has fled. Like ancient cities built on the rubble of previous cities, modern doubt is built upon the discarded theories of the past.

This is what Peter called "destructive heresies" (2 Pet. 2:1). The Book of Revelation tells us about "three unclean spirits like frogs coming out of the mouth of the dragon out of the mouth of the beast, and out of the mouth of the false prophet" (Rev. 16:13). They are a trinity of untruth. The Bible does not speak of a few church members being misled only. It speaks about nations, the whole world, heading for Armageddon.

That is where the gift of the discerning of spirits is needed. As believers we will increasingly find ourselves out of step with society, not "politically correct," because the world is deceived. The gift of the discerning of spirits will guide us in our walk through dangerous minefields. The Holy Spirit is the Spirit of truth, leading us into all truth, as Jesus promised. The believer is the truth-bearer, and the church is the pillar and ground of the truth.

"Now the Spirit expressly says that in latter times some will depart from the faith, giving heed to deceiving spirits and doctrines of demons" (1 Tim. 4:1). Our first concern is not table rapping, poltergeists, or imaginary "green demons" to be coughed up, but it is the flood of error engulfing the church and the world. Exorcism has an important role in our work for God, but we do not fight demon untruth by exorcism; we fight it by preaching the Word of truth.

Finally, remember again that a gift is a manifestation of the Spirit that works as and when needed, just as does a word of wisdom, a word of knowledge, or a prophecy. How does it come? In all the ways in which other utterances come—by vision, dream, the Word of God, spontaneous, even unrealized. In short the Holy Spirit will lead us into all truth, not to make us intellectually great, but to safeguard the mind and soul of God's people. The means by which He sometimes does it is this—"to another the discerning of spirits."

CHAPTER 15

TONGUES AND INTERPRETATION

STANLEY H. FRODSHAM wrote *With Signs Following* in 1946 in which he quoted stories of people speaking in languages they have never heard or learned. Of course, critics have asserted that it is impossible and have written tongues off with the explanation that they were third- or fourth-hand legends. They would, wouldn't they? On the same grounds the miracles of the Bible are dismissed.

Robert Skinner, as editor of the Canadian *Pentecostal Evangel*, has written about several firsthand instances in *Redemption* magazine in September 1993. His father, fluent in Kiswahili, heard a young woman baptized in the Spirit speaking perfect Kiswahili, which she had never heard in her life and which he translated. His son Gary, whom I personally know, was home from Uganda that year at the Eastern Pentecostal Bible College. A student had a German visitor present who had been a Christian only two weeks. After the service she expressed her enjoyment and said what a pleasure it had been to hear someone praying in Russian, a language she understood, and also how good was the interpretation. Neither of the two speakers knew any Russian.

Robert Skinner mentions among other incidents twenty language students going along skeptically to a Pentecostal meeting and hearing several languages, including fluent Italian and Russian, spoken by people who knew nothing of those languages.

Most of this century it has been impossible to write about tongues except in defense. For those who may still be facing objections and critics, we record something of things said in that long struggle, as of course there will always be contrary views.

Of all gifts this has attracted the greatest interest—and opposition. The discovery that speaking in tongues is a valid Christian experience turned out to be epoch-making for the church. Tongues activated the present worldwide Holy Spirit emphasis and became the catalyst for an evangelistic thrust, which has eclipsed everything before it, both in enterprise and success.

Speaking with tongues is often given the Greek name *glossolalia*. Because there are various ideas about tongues, their origin, and what they are, we will first define what we mean in this book. "Tongues" are earthly or celestial languages, spoken only by believers, as the Holy Spirit gives them utterance. The speakers may not know what they are saying. Being spiritually empowered, interpretation must be by the same means.

If speaking in tongues takes place in worship, addressed to the whole company, an interpretation must follow. Mainly for that reason, it will be easier to consider the two gifts, tongues and interpretation, together for much of this chapter.

TONGUES IN SCRIPTURE

There are twenty-six references to tongues in the New Testament: one in Mark 16, four in Acts, and twenty-one in 1 Corinthians. This may seem few, considering the weight given to tongues in the modern charismatic-Pentecostal scene. However, references to prophecy often include tongues. On the Day of Pentecost, when the first disciples spoke with tongues and a vast crowd came together asking what it was all about, Peter explained "This [i.e., speaking with tongues] is what the prophet Joel spoke about. Your sons and daughters will prophesy." (See Acts 2:16–17.) Tongues were prophecy, and if understood by hearers, as on the Day of Pentecost, they are as much prophecy as tongues in English would be to English hearers. The same is true, of course, when tongues are followed by an interpretation, as is usual in worship services—they become prophesy.

The glossolalia is mentioned in only three books of the entire New Testament—in Mark, Acts, and 1 Corinthians— but that is not significant. Paul wrote a second letter to the

Corinthians and made no reference to tongues or any gift whatever. He also wrote about the Lord's Table, the central ordinance of the Christian faith, in a long passage in 1 Corinthians but never gave it a passing mention in the second letter, nor do any other books refer to it except the first three Gospels. Even the Gospel of John says nothing about it, just as it omits a dozen or so other important matters. New Testament writings were prompted by some special need or occasion and not usually to propound a comprehensive theology. Paul does, of course, give us much teaching on particular aspects of the faith, but not right across the whole scale of truth.

SAD LESSONS OF HISTORY

Everyone ought to be given the background to the present operation of tongues in millions of believers. For most of the twentieth century tongues were rejected, and even forbidden, despite 1 Corinthians 14:39 admonition "Do not forbid to speak with tongues." Curiously, when the same chapter says, "Let your women keep silent in the churches" (v. 34), it was given full weight and applied against women, but the command not to forbid tongues was ignored. There are still churches that silence women and tongues, thus showing a fine disregard for the whole of chapter 14, except the verse that suits them about women. They also separate that one verse from what Paul says on the same subject elsewhere. In this short chapter, however, we have no space to detail the back somersault of such theologians.

The "tongues people," as they were dubbed, were for decades the traditional targets needing the exhortations to love in 1 Corinthians 13. It is hard for us to see that such critical innuendos displayed much love or that the critics themselves were shining examples of that virtue. Of course, chapter 13 is the Word of God, and we should all take it to heart. It contains nine verses stressing love. However, what about the seventy-five verses in the same letter that encourage the use of gifts? Indeed, the love chapter itself is about gifts, including tongues (1 Cor. 13:1, 8), and was written to show the attitude in which tongues speaking should take place. Furthermore, it is followed immediately with the command "Desire spiritual gifts" (1 Cor. 14:1). Unfortunately the chapter heading destroys the connected thought. Can we give serious attention to the love chapter and ignore the gift of tongues, which the love chapter is about?

Those who saw and accepted tongues at the beginning of the twentieth century were some of the most devout and godly Bible-preaching people, products in fact of the holiness movement itself. They were passionately concerned with world evangelism, and after they accepted the Pentecostal blessing in 1901, a soul-saving revival was soon well on the way, which has spanned the century unabated.

The history of the glossolalia from the beginning of the first day of the twentieth century is full of spiritual significance.

It has produced the greatest soul-saving witness in the entire Christian age. However, the evangelical world conjured up a real fear of tongues, and leaders massed their weight against it. That was tragic and had far-reaching consequences. God had sent revival, but it was rejected by millions of biblical Christians. Apostolic-style revival made its own way mainly without evangelical encouragement. When George Jeffreys, the greatest and earliest of British Pentecostal evangelists, the man I mentioned laying hands on me, went through the United Kingdom like a flame of fire, warnings against him went out from almost every church pulpit. In Britain's second largest city, Birmingham, ten thousand people received Christ, and one thousand testimonies of healing were received, yet a leading free churchman tried to organize a counter-attraction against him.

That position changed only when the era of the charismatic renewal began in the late 1950s and '60s. The nations, which could have been swept by revival if the moving of the Spirit in this new way had been accepted by evangelicals, were swept by war. This sad rejection of biblical gifts was incomprehensible. Slanderous and false reports were a main reason. The enemy and "accuser of the brethren" made fear his major strategy. The devil could see what damage a miraculous gospel would do to his infernal kingdom. In fact, the very zeal of the "tongues people" to win others for Christ actually deepened alarm among Bible-believers and also liberals. The most godly leaders were misled by the general reports, prejudice, and also by practical pressures. To accept tongues would have put one of the most eminent evangelicals outside the camp and no doubt outside his church.

In 1904 the Welsh revival began. It created almost desperate hunger worldwide for such blessing. In Germany the evangelicals organized conventions and prayer efforts. The cry was, "Lord, do it again." The revival visualized was a repeat of the Wesley-Whitefield-Edwards awakenings. But God wanted to do a new thing and waited.

In Germany an evangelical leader with no charismatic experience began experimental services for the baptism in the Spirit, which drew a mixed multitude of wonder seekers, many of dubious religious stock. Things were allowed to get out of hand, and two experienced Pentecostal women brought in from Norway to help went home disgusted.

The damage was far reaching and spawned the infamous "Berlin Declaration," denouncing the tongues movement as "from below," of the devil.[1] This short document was merely assertive and contained not a single argument, scriptural or otherwise. Most German evangelicals, under threat of disfellowship, had to toe the line it laid down. Thus the Declaration rooted itself deeply and bore bitter fruit.

Today, praise God, as I write, I personally have found a new attitude in Germany and everywhere else among evangelicals toward the charismatic-Pentecostal revival. The leaves of the one-hundred-year-old Declaration are yellowing, and an attitude of Christian love is slowly wiping out past misunderstanding. Perhaps this may be the passing forever of those tragic days and the Declaration.

It should, I think, also be recorded that, not surprisingly, many within the revival eased their foot off the spiritual accelerator, shy of persecution. There was a general desire not to offend the mainline church by ostentatious tongues, and often it was thought foolish to mention such a strange practice too publicly. Eventually the charismatic renewal movement began bringing release from this and other inhibiting cautions.

THE BASIC PROBLEM

The foregoing will, we hope, help a new generation to understand the background to any lingering hesitations about tongues. There are many who have no objections when others speak in tongues, but they are not keen about it for themselves. Is it possible to be Pentecostal or charismatic without speaking with tongues? Well, on the first truly Pentecostal day they all spoke with tongues. Other supernatural gifts are fine—healing, casting out demons, prophecy, wisdom, knowledge, and miracles. There is a difference: none of these require quite the same self-surrender. They can operate while we keep our best coat buttoned up in dignity. We can indeed heal the sick and give forth wisdom, knowledge, and prophecies all quite majestically, but speaking with tongues is different. We can receive even salvation with propriety, but tongues seem to be a humbling of our dignity and composure. Maybe that is why God gives them.

Many Christians have been brought up with anti-tongues attitudes and have been conditioned against the practice. Others have been disillusioned. Those using artificial methods of inducing tongues have done considerable damage. But the core is fear, a psychological instinct to hold on to ourselves, whereas to speak with tongues looks too much like losing control—it is supposed. This is a needless fear. God never takes over like that and robs us of our will.

According to Acts 2:4, "they…began to speak with other tongues, as the Spirit gave them utterance." When the will of man and the will of God come together in balance, then and only then is utterance possible. We need not be afraid of being "taken over," and we should never allow it. The baptism in the Spirit is not to be described as being possessed by the Holy Spirit. It is not Spirit possession. A demon may render people possessed, but not the blessed Spirit of God. We should, of course, recognize that God has a right to us as temples and as His servants—"I beseech you therefore, brethren, by the mercies of God, that you present your bodies a living sacrifice, holy, acceptable to God, which is your reasonable service" (Rom. 12:1).

If we want the Holy Spirit, then we should remember what Peter says: "Holy men of God spoke as they were moved by the Holy Spirit" (2 Pet. 1:21). They had no qualms about it, no worries about being "possessed" or about keeping their self-possession and dignity. Dignity is not one of the fruit of the Spirit anyway, but joy is! God never wrests control, yet He does need to come into the flesh and share in the business of our speech. As for dignity, if we want what the apostles got, they did not stand on their dignity too much. They were mocked and said to be drunk on the Day of Pentecost. But that is a small cost for such a big benefit.

Our real handicap is pure instinct: "I am me, and nobody else is going to get so close to me that anything I do is not completely me. Not even God." We zip our souls up and regard the Holy Spirit as an intruder. He wants to make our bodies His temple. That is the trouble—it is just our bodies that we are so fussy about maintaining inviolate.

The Spirit of God has not come to violate. It is not an invasion—we were made for His indwelling, and Dr. Huxley's remark is more true than he realized, that "there is a God-shaped vacuum in our soul." Only God can fill it. That is the crux of the matter. The human heart has a golden gate that will never be opened except for the Lord of hosts, like that of Jerusalem.

God wants us not only spiritually but also physically—that is the revolution of Pentecost, and that is the Rubicon so many fear to cross while admiring those who have. Physically and in every way we are to be one with Him, we in Him and He in us, like a sponge in water. A cloth in purple dye takes on the character of the element into which it is dipped. So do those baptized in the Spirit.

If then He dwells in us physically, should there not be a physical sign? What else but speaking with tongues? Is not the tongue like a rudder that steers the ship, as James says? (See James 3.) Then what does it mean when we do not let God use our tongues to speak with? If the gift is from Him, if we speak with tongues as the Spirit gives utterance, could it be anything but wonderful?

The glorious experience of being swept into the ocean of God's purposes, carried along (like the prophets of Israel) in that Pentecostal mighty rushing wind—is that what we are afraid of? Has the starch of what we call civilization stiffened our garb and turned into steel armor, so that it has become difficult to "put on Christ"? Where are His tears? Where His passion? Where our cross bearing? Where His total unself-consciousness and yieldedness to God? The world admires every passionate enthusiasm except one, love for God. What do we want? Do we want our cozy culture and sophistication—or the burning and palpitating drive of the divine nature?

There does not appear to be any wide recognition of the fact that the baptism in the Spirit with tongues is a truth that enhances all other truths. A new dimension is opened to us not only in life but also in theology and every relationship. Truth shines more brilliantly at every turn of the jewel—God in the flesh, not just "spiritually." Joel had said the Spirit would be poured out on all flesh. God comes upon us in our flesh as well as our spirit.

Whether we speak about salvation, forgiveness, or redemption, the flesh is involved—even when we speak of God, for "the Word became flesh" (John 1:14). There is no way that the divine oneness with our human nature could now be better demonstrated than when the Spirit gives utterance with us. The presence of God in His people has always affected them vocally. Theologians have now to think in terms of what happened at Pentecost or miss the key to an enlarged library of truth. If the only perfect Man who ever lived was a divine-human union, and we are destined to be like Him, why shun any evidence of it in the present day? The fullness of the Godhead indwelt Him bodily.

THE GIFT OF GOD

The Pentecostals in their little storefront churches and backstreet halls stuck to their guns for half a century of contempt. Those church groups, now numbering 220 million, usually write tongues in their Fundamentals as the sign of the baptism in the Spirit. Whatever arguments are used, whether Acts was intended to teach theology or not, the record is enough. The Bible way of being full of the Spirit and knowing it is clear enough. It was always with outward manifestations, and the only one invariably mentioned is tongues. Nobody but nobody in apostolic days had it any other way.

If people do not like tongues, how do they propose they will know they have the Holy Spirit? How will it show in their personality? Going around healing others does not show how we ourselves are blessed. We are talking about new creatures, not old creatures made a little livelier, but life from the dead.

Tongues are the only gift named in every list in 1 Corinthians 12–14. Tongues—real tongues—would be impossible without God. It is a gift from heaven. Should anybody protect and defend themselves against it? In an earlier chapter we said that there is no such thing as greater and lesser gifts. There is also no such thing as a gift of so little consequence that it need not interest us. God does not give trivial gifts. If we cannot see their value, He does.

There are those who teach that we can be filled with the Spirit without tongues, or even that we receive the Spirit at new birth and seek the gifts afterward. It eliminates the need for the Pentecostal "initial evidence" of tongues. Well, why is such teaching so welcome? No tongues—what attraction is that? If you do not bother with this gift, another will have to be crossed out of the Corinthian list—interpretation. Are we superior to what God offers?

TONGUES IN OPERATION

Literature on tongues would fill a library. In this book we are attempting to set down guidance, understanding, and something more. The object is to stimulate the desire for the God-given gifts, which have always proved to come hand in hand with faith and evangelistic vision.

The "tongues people" are becoming a major factor in

history, secular and religious, simply because of their eagerness to see others turn to God. There is a bright fire in their soul, a conviction that runs deep. Do not ask how or why. It is there. Perhaps others have it too, but certainly millions would not have it at all unless speaking with tongues had introduced to them the indwelling Spirit.

Earlier we referred to the fact that the nine manifestations, which Paul describes in list one of 1 Corinthians 12, are not all there are. This is a quick list of gifts that particularly affect Christian worship. Other works of the Spirit, such as casting out demons, taking up serpents, and immunity to poison, are not part of normal worship.

Paul ranks prophecy higher than did the Corinthians, who preferred the more showy manifestations, especially tongues. The love of the sensational is not unknown in any age, and it is evident enough today. The miraculous may be sought purely because it is sensational. Speaking with tongues in Corinth sounded to Paul like "sounding brass or a clanging cymbal" (1 Cor. 13:1), sounding off and showing off. This proud accomplishment Paul suddenly reduces to dependency on a prophesier, saying a tongues man is not to speak at all without an interpretation.

INTERPRETATION

The Greek word used for "interpretation" in 1 Corinthians 12:10 is *hermeneia*. The experts tell us that this means "to explain what is said" rather than translate. In 1 Corinthians

14:27–28, it is similar; i.e., to put into words (Greek: *diermeneuo*).

We would like to offer some help and guidelines, especially as tongues used publicly is expected to be in the context of worship. What may be concisely expressed by the Spirit in one language may need more explaining in English. We know nothing about the tongues of angels, which could be much more concise than our languages, needing many earth-language words to interpret them. A brief utterance in tongues, followed by an interpretation five times as long, may have another explanation, namely, a prophetic development of the same theme continuing in the spirit of prophecy.

The interpretation does not need to take place as soon as the tongues speaker has ceased. The whole service does not need to be quieted waiting for the interpreter to begin. There is no reason why it should not be given later. For that matter, it could be even given in a subsequent meeting if the Spirit allows it and the same congregation is present, though that would be rare.

It has been said that some utterances in tongues are only praise to God and need no interpretation. But why not interpret praise? Tongues and interpretation have a worship quality, and praise is edifying. Those who understood the languages spoken on the Day of Pentecost heard them speak "the wonderful works of God" (Acts 2:11). That is like the Psalms. Why not now?

The wonderful works of God before Christ were described

in the Psalms as His miracle acts, such as the deliverance from Egypt. Worship should not be mainly about bowing before a heavenly (and unimaginable) throne in heaven. The wonderful work of God was that "God was in Christ reconciling the world to Himself" (2 Cor. 5:19). Calvary has always been the Christian theme. So when speaking with tongues is interpreted, the great salvation spoken of by the prophets will, not surprisingly, be the theme of modern prophets. The glory of the Cross and the supreme work of God written in blood at Calvary were the subject of praise in glory when John saw what was going on there (Rev. 5).

To say that Paul discourages tongues is one of the most remarkable instances of turning Scripture on its head I have ever known. First Corinthians 14 makes statements about tongues that are not made even about prophecy. "He who speaks in a tongue does not speak to men but to God" (v. 2). "In the spirit he speaks mysteries" (v. 2). "If I pray in a tongue, my spirit prays" (v. 14). "Tongues are for a sign...to unbelievers" (v. 22). You are praising God with your spirit.

SERVICE ORDER

The Corinthian instructions end with verses 39 and 40 in chapter 14: "Therefore, brethren, desire earnestly to prophesy, and do not forbid to speak with tongues. Let all things be done decently and in order." What order? Ours or God's? Our cast-iron structured proceedings? That is not indicated at all. God's order may have an alpine ruggedness about it and still retain an aspect of grandeur. Worship can have spontaneity, the mountain surprise view. "Whenever you come together, each one of you has a psalm, has a teaching, has a tongue, has a revelation, has an interpretation" (v. 26). This is Holy Spirit worship, rivers of living water and streams in the desert.

However, speaking with tongues is not confined to use in church. Paul wishes that they all spoke with tongues. Obviously not everybody could give an utterance when gathered for worship (vv. 5, 23). There would not be time, unless they stayed a week. Paul's wish for all to speak with tongues could only be realized if people exercised their fluency in private worship.

Speaking in tongues is prayer (v. 2) and is therefore one way in which to "pray in the Spirit," especially when "we do not know what we should pray for," as Romans 8:26 says. It is interesting that this applies not necessarily to praying for someone else but also for ourselves, for it continues, "The Spirit Himself makes intercession for us." We pray for ourselves when we pray in tongues. This explains why millions find themselves "getting through" when the mood seems to be missing in prayer if they take advantage of this manifestation in their lives. However, Paul is mainly concerned with tongues in public worship.

It is in the church that Paul visualizes the operation of the gifts for "edification and exhortation and comfort" (1 Cor. 14:3), and any prophecy should be proved by others. These two instructions make it very clear that tongues, interpretation, and prophecy are not for private guidance, nor for the family circle, nor between friends, nor between husband and wife. This kind of thing should take place in the congregation where there are others to judge.

Experience has shown how important this is. The practice of using tongues and interpretation privately in the home, more particularly to obtain guidance, does not need to be described as inadvisable—it has brought calamity and shipwreck. It is a way to divide churches. There must be others to judge, which means that oversight is needed even in church worship.

WHAT ARE TONGUES?

Tongues have been explained as psychological, being "thrown up from the subconscious mind under mental stress." It amazes me that such fantastic abilities are attributed to the subconscious mind—that people can utter lengthy and intelligible speeches in languages they have never heard and even describe in tongues matters completely outside their knowledge.

Nils Bloch Hoel's *The Pentecostal Movement* (1964), diagnoses tongues speaking as a psychological illness and tongues speakers as a subspecies. His medical opinion is that "real xenolalia" (foreign languages) is some sort of mental lapse, when long forgotten foreign phrases are released in "motoric speech" when the patient is in a state of ecstasy or trauma. He wraps this far-fetched nonsense around with high-sounding jargon, hypermnesia or cryptomnesia, and considers that a "satisfactory rational explanation." Nothing could be less "satisfactory" or "rational."

Those of us who speak with tongues daily can state that it is not done in an ecstasy or trauma and that we are in full control of our mental state. Nils Bloch Hoel, however, is himself not so sure he has explained things, for he adds that future investigation in psychology may come forward with some different explanation. Indeed, yes—the Holy Spirit perhaps? Why not? And that is an explanation nobody can disprove.

By way of answer we can mention another Norwegian, Thoralf Gilbrant, a scholar and international editor of the sixteen-volume *The Complete Biblical Library*. In 1985, at the Pentecostal World Conference, he testified that his grandmother had preached to Italian ship crews in fluent Italian, not knowing a word of it, and he himself heard an elderly choir man praying in beautiful British English, not American. Later, assuming the man had lived there, he struck up a conversation and discovered he knew no English whatsoever. The choir man was not in a state of ecstasy, trauma, or anything approaching it.

Others think that it was a very special, one-off miracle on the Day of Pentecost, when the 120 spoke with recognizable languages that they had never learned, and that the tongues in Corinth were quite different. There is not only no evidence whatsoever for such an idea but also no value in the idea either, except to push back the miraculous into more remote history.

An objection has been raised that tongues have been heard among those who are not Christians. Mormons can produce their own cases of tongues. No doubt. In fact, as mentioned earlier, the oracles at the temples of pagan gods sometimes gave forth their pronouncements in gibberish through the lips of vestal virgins, which priests purported to interpret. The devil, like the magicians of Egypt, can counterfeit the miracles of God and supernaturally impart utterances. That was expected by Paul in 1 Corinthians 12:3: "No one speaking by the Spirit of God calls Jesus accursed." Paul was not inventing a hypothetical possibility. It could happen, and possibly did, but it would be by another spirit other than from God. The occult is supernatural, as are the gifts of the Spirit.

That Satan can produce phenomena does not mean that all phenomena are satanic. Jesus was meeting such a fear when He said:

> If a son asks for bread from any father among you, will he give him a stone? Or if he asks for a fish, will he give him a serpent instead of a fish?...If you then, being evil, know how to give good gifts to your children, how much more will your heavenly Father give the Holy Spirit to those who ask Him!
>
> —LUKE 11:11–13

Speaking with tongues has sometimes been more baffling to unbelief and more convincing to the unprejudice, than healing and visible miracles.

The question of what the gift of tongues is can now be easily answered. Not everybody who speaks with tongues is gifted for their use in public worship—which Paul was concerned with in 1 Corinthians. If certain people in a church seem to be prominent in this utterance, that is how it should be. "Gift" has more than one meaning. Speaking with tongues is a gift of God in the general sense, but in the church sense, the gift has come to the man or woman who frequently feels a special inspiration to edify the congregation in this way—with an interpreter, fulfilling the law "By the mouth of two or three witnesses every word shall be established" (2 Cor. 13:1).

TONGUES THAT AID US

Let us now enumerate the ways in which we are helped by speaking with tongues.

- They are an utterance in prayer for needs we cannot ourselves express and do not know how to pray. They enable us to sense the presence of God and know that He is bending to hear us.

- Demon hindrance is overcome.

- When our minds can no longer concentrate, our spirit prays.

- We can pray in tongues when we are otherwise having to concentrate upon some mechanical task, such as driving a car.

- We edify ourselves.

We leave this important subject at this juncture, though it deserves far lengthier examination. The Spirit of God is seeking every way to break through into our needy lives and our desperate world. May we be open to His partnership!

CHAPTER 16

DIVIDED TONGUES
AS OF FIRE

Hebrews 1:7 states, "[God] makes His angels spirits and His ministers a flame of fire." A successful church is a burning bush. God speaks from it. Our word is His word, or it is no word at all. A church aflame with God, a bush burning with holy fire will attract people better than any amount of PR hype. The eminent Swiss theologian Emil Brunner said, "The church exists by mission as fire exists by burning." It burns by mission.

We want forests of burning bushes. God is clothed with fire, and His servants are "flames of fire." Unless we are burning, we can never set anybody else on fire. Martyrius Sadna complained, "We stand laxly in his presence as though it were just a game." Is that true of any of us here?

We can be so orderly, doing everything with dignity and decorum...but without fire! In other words, correct but cold.

On Mount Carmel the pagans laid everything correctly on the altar ready for the sacrifice, but the devil could not bring a spark from hell to light it. Elijah then rebuilt the altar—stones, wood, sacrifice, everything according to the book—and called down fire from heaven. And it came!

FERVOR OR FAILURE

Fire is the divine logo. Like it or lump it, the Christian faith is either fervent or a failure. It is characterised by fire: hearts and lives ablaze, faces glowing with God, alight with fervor and enthusiasm. Scripture has more than one hundred references to the fire of God.

Fire also announces the presence of the Lord. "Our God comes…and a fire devours before him" (Ps. 50:3, NIV). His banner is fire. Each tribe of Israel had its banner as they marched through the desert on their way to the Promised Land, but at their head was the pillar of fire, God's banner and the emblem of the nation.

In New Testament times the same emblem was at hand. John the Baptist declared the most distinctive truth about Jesus. He announced that Jesus would baptize in the Holy Spirit and fire. That fiery baptism was what would identify the Messiah. So even before Jesus actually appeared on the scene, people were told to expect fire. That is what the faith is, fire!

The Christian church is first and foremost a bringer of fire, a blazing torch to set light to the land. Only faith in

God can give the world an overriding objective. The world's passions are greed, lust, and power, but only dedication to Christ can girdle the globe with a living purpose. Only the passions of Jesus can set the mountains ablaze. In Britain people celebrated the end of World War II by lighting beacons on the high hills from the south to the north and from east to west. Each beacon was lit as the people caught sight of the next one down the line, a chain of victory fires with flames billowing in the hilltop winds. That is how it works for Christians—be on fire, and others will catch it. Like the sun, God is big enough to go to for fire. If you are on fire for God, never mind the winds of adversity. Wind blows only candles out; it makes fires brighter. Churches are intended to be beacons on hilltops, not candles in the cellar.

FIRE—THE MOST VIVID ATTRACTION

The only fireless religion in Scripture is false religion with its false fire. Some are obessed with religion only. Frenzy is not fire, nor is fanaticism, a hothead, or an overheated mind. At the opposite extreme, scholars and human opinion form the basis of many churches. Critical scholars are often rather like fire brigades—adept at putting the fire out. Their interests are academic, coolheadedly devoid of passion for the gospel. Their gospel does not have the intensity of Paul's messages. Theologians, teachers, and preachers like that never stir anyone's heart and never create eagerness for God or the gospel.[1]

Major churches in medieval times were called after their

patron saint. For a church to be named after a saint often meant that it was in possession of a relic or two, usually a bone from the saint's body. The name rested on a dead man or woman. Their faith and hopes of help rested on a bone! Imagine: blessing by bones, faith by relics!

I was thinking of Peter and John at the tomb examining the grave clothes of the risen Christ. It never even crossed their minds that they might display the blood-marked wrappings as evidence of His death, like holy relics to be kissed and touched. They had better things to do! In fact, they spent their time waiting in the Upper Room until the fire fell. Pentecost is not a token of death but a trophy of life and victory. The true sign of a living Lord is living fire from heaven. As they looked at the disciples, even enemies could tell that they had been with Jesus. We need scholarship like we need every kind of help from one another, but how much better it is when it comed from *flame people*, the Spirit kindling their thoughts.

In a Spanish village they had a saint—alive. The people were worried in case he left them, so they killed him and kept his bones to ensure that his blessing did not go away! Relics only prove death. Pieces of the cross signified only that Jesus had died! People are not drawn by symbols of death but of life. The true "relics" of Christ are flame people, not a piece of cloth, not the canonized dead, but living, Spirit-baptized people. The proof, signs, and evidence that Jesus rose from death are living people with the abounding life that He promised. Because He lives, we live too—by the power of immortal life.

This year is the centenary anniversary of the Welsh revival. In a matter of months some one hundred thousand people were converted and joined the chapels. The chapels were like fireplaces. Little of them is left today. Those fireplaces are full of cold ash and cinders. Chapels where strong men on their knees repented in tears are now used as bingo halls or warehouses. The glory and the fire have gone, "Ichabod" is written across church doors, chapels are empty, but the prisons are full again. Revival completely eliminated crime, but apostasy has produced the highest crime rate ever recorded. God wants furnaces; He doesn't want freezers.

THEOLOGY OF PENTECOST

The divided tongues of Holy Spirit fire are the assurance that He is with us. Two of the greatest spiritual crises were inaugurated by divine fire, namely the Exodus and Pentecost. Yet for the birth, life, death, and resurrection of Christ there was no fire. It was not needed. The baptizer in fire was present Himself—infinitely greater than the fire symbolizing His presence. Fire, you might say, is His logo…and so much more! When Jesus ascended to the right hand of God, the fire fell on ordinary human beings. It enables us to witness for Jesus, to show Him to be as He is. Any fire that does not bring Him close and generate love for Him is not His fire.

The promised Holy Spirit is dedicated to the task of revealing the things of Christ to us. Where the fire is, there is Jesus.

The theology of the Ascension is the theology of Pentecost. When Christ ascended to heaven, it was to a special place: "the right hand of God" (Mark 16:19). The right hand is the hand of power and authority. Scripture always speaks of the right hand or right arm. Jesus was God's right hand. In fact, we never read of God's left hand. The left hand was the place of shame and failure. (See Matthew 25:33.) Only once do we read about the arms of the Lord (Deut. 33:27). It is otherwise always the arm or hand of the Lord. The arm of the Lord is the Lord, the Son of God. A father's right arm was always his son. God broke Pharaoh's arm when his firstborn son died (Ezek. 30:21). Psalm 89:13 tells us that God's arm "is endued with power." When the world and the devil launched their attacks against Christ, it was against the right hand of God, which could never be broken.

"The LORD will lay bare his holy arm in the sight of all the nations, and all the ends of the earth will see the salvation of our God" (Isa. 52:10, NIV). That prophecy was fulfilled when Christ came to earth. The aged man Simeon saw the child Jesus when He was taken to the temple for the first time. He blessed Him, saying, "Lord...my eyes have seen Your salvation which You have prepared before the face of all peoples" (Luke 2:29–31). Jesus is salvation, our salvation, the mighty arm of God made bare to save us. Rather than to destroy enemies, for God to bare His arm is salvation. When Christ rose to be the right hand of God, the first thing He did was to send the fire of Pentecost.

SIMULATED FIRES

There are false fires. The fire in which the voice of Jesus is heard, that is the real one. In chilly Britain, homes are warmed by simulated coal fires. People used to burn real coal in their fireplaces, and houses had chimneys. The fireplaces and chimneys are still there, but the fire comes from gas jets—no burning coals, no faces in the fire, no toast at the bars, no kettle singing on the hob. Some houses, like most apartments in continental Europe, have no gas fire and are heated by central heating radiators, with circulated hot water. Radiators are deadpan, unsmiling, never glowing, never radiant—just a lot of hot water. Jesus, however, did not come to baptize in water—hot or cold—but in fire, real fire, not simulated.

Church religion is full of symbolism. The presence of God is suggested through architecture, music, vestments, tone of voice, furniture, or noisy groups and drums. Churches baptize in water but not in the Holy Spirit and fire. We may all need some physical helps to worship, but the impulse itself must be fire in our belly. The song reaching heaven does not come from lips but hearts.

Preaching too can be so well educated, so slick, so well honed and professional, the right gesture at the right time, the right story, the right cadence of voice, the tear and the sob at the appropriate place, the appropriate shout, the rising oratorical crescendo, flourishes and climaxes, with the cue for the choir to come in at the critical moment. Certainly nothing is to be condemned if it provokes and brings forth God's praise, but if not, it is not a burning bush. A church may represent a beautiful and cultivated shrub, but it should be a bush aflame, speaking the passion of God.

It were not kings, poets, and intellectuals that filled the pages of Scripture, but people with a burning heart, every one—Noah, Abraham, Jacob, Joseph, Moses, Joshua, David, Elijah, Elisha, Daniel, Ezekiel, the many Marys of the Gospels, and the women Paul greeted in Romans 16. They had no qualms about emotionalism. God had set them on fire, and they just burned and blazed on. God's call was not for cool customers, people composed and without feeling. They were enthusiasts, every one of them. Israel began with charismatic Spirit-strengthened leaders but ended with pagan kings.

Jesus said of John the Baptist that he was a "lamp that burned and gave light" (John 5:35, NIV). I would rather be a John burning and giving light than be a king! King Herod in his palace shed no light on the path of the world, while John the Baptist in Herod's palace dungeon still blazes away today. Nero lit his palace gardens by binding Christians in leather and pitch and setting them on fire. Today dogs are called Nero, and the flame of those martyrs is inextinguishable.

FIREPLACES

The human heart is a fireplace made to hold fire. There are too many cold grates, many of them ash cans, like dustbins, full of rubbish. Years ago when fireplaces were made of iron, housewives used to spend a considerable amount of time and effort polishing the grates. In the hungry 1930s they had no coal and no fire, but they polished away. Could churches be described as "1930s style"—polished sermons but no fire?

God took an ordinary bush and set it ablaze. He made it extraordinary before He spoke from it. God does not normally speak out of bushes, however beautiful they may be. Until He visited that wilderness, that bush was unremarkable. Moses had seen it before but hardly noticed it. Yet when the flames of heaven were kindled in it, it was no longer unremarkable. The same goes for churches! The world has no respect for a church of sanctimonious milk-and-water sentiments, wishy-washy philosophy, pretty thoughts, and uncertainties. If a church at least burns for God, it will attract notice. When churches are models of decency, decorum, conformity, and correctness, nobody says, "I will now turn aside and see this great sight" (Exod. 3:3). When there is a spiritual blaze, people stop and stare.

FIRE MAKES FAMOUS

Bushes should not burn, and many supposed churches should not burn either! If they do, somebody will look for a fire extinguisher. A church that burns is not normal. It is spectacular, and people stop to look. Some who stop will be like Moses and hear the voice of God, though others will be deaf. However, that is where God separates the people of the past from the people of the future. The past spelled Egypt, bondage. The fire spelled freedom, adventure, and life. People are not seeking perfection but fire, warmth, and passion. Churches may look opulent, popular, and, successful, but I think of Peter and John. They had to confess, "Silver or gold I do not have" (Acts 3:6). They were both too shabby to attract admiration, but they could continue, "But what I do have I give you: In the name of Jesus Christ of Nazareth, rise up and walk." They did not have any cash, but they did have God.

Fire made the bush the most famous bush that ever grew. Only Moses saw it, but nobody can forget it. Fire made it what it was, and it made Moses who he was. He was learned in all the wisdom of Egypt, but for all that he would have died a nobody, a dusty mummy in Egypt. Yet he met the God of fire in the wilderness, and he matters today very much. Similarly, the disciples were unknowns, fishing workers, until the tongues of flame rested upon them, and soon they had turned the world upside down. They did not know themselves until the fire transformed them. Their fervor brought them persecution and plenty of verbal abuse, but they are remembered and their persecutors are lost in oblivion. If any preacher hopes to be noted and remembered, let him be a burning bush.

FIRE ENDS DIVISION

The divided tongues brought an end to division. Even when they were following Jesus, the disciples vied with one another to see who should be greatest. After Pentecost, however, we read that they "devoted themselves...to the fellowship....All the believers were together and had everything in common....They broke bread in their homes and ate together" (Acts 2:42–46, NIV). One fire was divided into many flames, yet each was the fire of God. They did not need two flames for double power. Those divided flames created a new breed of men—not clones of one another but one new race, a new people. One flame represented the entire fire of God. Andrew's flame burned with a different color than James's fire. John was still John, but he became a flame called John. Thomas became an on-fire Thomas. Flame people! People who have dwelt with the everlasting burnings cannot stand smoldering smoke. The disciples were called when they were like black candlewicks, but the love of Christ lit them. Candles in a box, tossed into a corner—but taken out and set alight, they lit up the world!

MORE OF GOD?

Our real self, our true personality, is dead until lit by the fire of God. Then we become what God meant us to be, each one blessed and filled with the same fullness. We are all made to drink the same blessing, and yet each of us represents the whole. O this glorious fullness of the Spirit, joy, fire, glory! To be baptized in the Spirit means that the Spirit is in us and we are in the Spirit. Like a cloth in dye, the dye is in the cloth. When it is dipped into the color, it takes on the nature of the dye.

People talk about getting more of God, more Holy Spirit. More? If we are in the ocean, we are wet and cannot get more wet. We are wet with the whole Pacific, the whole Atlantic of the Spirit, not dampened by a drop from a child's seaside bucket. The wetness, the water that clings to us stretches to the shoreless reaches of God. We are one in the Spirit with all who bathe in those waters. "For we were all baptized by one Spirit into one body...and we were all given the one Spirit to drink" (1 Cor. 12:13, NIV).[2]

FIRE FOR DELIVERANCE

God's first personal revelation to anybody was to Moses, and it was as fire. Then Moses was commissioned to set his people free. "He makes...his servants flames of fire" (Heb. 1:7, NIV), not to show off but to secure the release of captives. The word from the bush was a word of deliverance from the God of salvation. His voice established His attitude and His character.

Deliverance is God's most important business, as we know Him. It took a week to make heaven and earth, but it took

Christ a lifetime to bring salvation. To put fire in the hearts of the disciples, He tore open the very heavens. With the wind He ripped a path through the Red Sea for Israel's deliverance, and with the same tornado from heaven He arrived in the Upper Room to escort the disciples on their way to deliver millions of the devil's enslaved victims. His greatest revelation about Himself to us is that He is the deliverer. Whatever else He is, perhaps in other universes, angels may know, but He is too great for us to contemplate in entirety. It is enough to know Him as He is toward this sinful world, and that is as the Lord of liberty, the God of emancipation.

God shows us what He is to make us what He wants us to be. He does not talk about Himself to impart information but always for transformation. His Word to us is quickening, shaping us and fashioning us into His likeness. He wants us to be like Him, the supreme aim and reward of existence. When He turned heaven and earth upside down, it was for our salvation. He comes to us now, taps us on the shoulder, and says, "I want you. Come and help Me to sort out the mess the devil has made." By all means, save some by all means. Save! Save! What a great Bible word! A Bible invitation.

Make no mistake about, if the fire of God touches us, it is to make us witnesses to the very ends of the earth. The baptism in the Spirit is not heavenly candy handed to you by a doting Father, a sugar lollipop, but it is spiritual muscle, fiber, and stamina to set you up in business for God, a soul-saving business. The church is not a social club but the blazing chariot of God.

The Bible too is our fire guide. God did not provide a textbook for scholars. On the other hand, Bible study is not meant to be a hobby, like learning a language or a pleasant read on a quiet Sunday afternoon. It is always about deliverance and to set us on our chief business. God is on fire to save, the God of salvation. His plan in Pentecost is for us to burn as He burns, burning to bring salvation to the world. God does not come from heaven as an emotional stimulant, to warm us a little, give us good meetings, and send us home happy. The Spirit is not concerned with our feelings but with the state of mankind. We may be affected emotionally by His presence, perhaps enraptured, but that is incidental. The purpose of God's Spirit coming in among us is to send us out.

LIBERALITY WITHOUT A CALCULATOR

"An offering made by fire…to the Lord" (Lev. 2:9)—words like that occur time after time in Leviticus. Fire offerings. The question is not about what we are giving Him but how. Are we eager and work and give for the pleasure it gives us? If it brings us satisfaction, it will satisfy God. When you bring a gift to your spouse, it is a joy. We are to delight in God, and giving is part of that delight. A love gift is a live gift.

God wants no cold offerings. Isaiah 1:13 tells us, "Stop bringing meaningless offerings!" (NIV). What made those offerings meaningless? Well, it is simple, really. The people presented offerings as an obligation, to fulfill the religious law. Their heart was not in it. To them it was merely a legal requirement; therefore it could never bring God satisfaction. Their offerings were empty formalities, whereas God wanted love gifts, signs of their heart worship, their privilege and joy.

God has never demanded gifts. What value would they be to Him, given under duress? He leaves the whole business of giving to us. That is our affair, to do what we want, and that pleases God—an offering made to the Lord by fire.

Paul says that to offer ourselves is our "reasonable service" (Rom. 12:1); in other words, a natural, appropriate, and spontaneous reaction. Seeing who we are and what God has done with us, the normal human impulse is eager response, the kind of gift you would give a spouse whom you love dearly. Forced gifts will afford God no pleasure—only what comes from an overflowing heart can do that.

I am amazed when somebody tries to prove from Scripture that there is a law of tithing! A law? Is that how God goes about things, ordering us to give to Him? God is not a taxman, not a shylock demanding his legal pound of flesh. People say that they tithe by God's command. Can you imagine God grabbing what He made you give? Should a Christian give by compulsion? If tithing were only a scriptural necessity, what value would it be in God's eyes? The Pharisees gave like that, but Jesus thought nothing of it at all! "God loves a cheerful giver," we are told (2 Corinthians

9:7). I do not know anyone who gives cheerfully because he is forced to!

Tithing, giving, is a love opportunity, an expression of heartfelt worship, a love compulsion not a legal requirement. The idea of giving a tenth, is that Christian giving? Calculating and careful? It is not called for in the New Testament—not after we saw how God gave and how Christ gave. The Lord wants an offering made by fire—generosity on fire from a life on fire, liberality without a calculator. You can give a tithe or whatever you like, but let it be an offering made to the Lord by fire.

ONE FINAL WORD

John the Baptist declared that the One who was to come would baptize in the Holy Spirit and fire. That was the key message and the way to identify Christ. Interestingly, however, Jesus baptized nobody in fire while He was on earth. John was therefore perhaps justified in asking whether Jesus was the one that he had been expecting, seeing that Jesus did not fulfill the prophecy about fire. But Jesus said, "Blessed is the man who does not fall away on account of me" (Luke 7:23, NIV). The prophecy was not intended for the short term of Christ's days on earth. It had a far greater anticipation, a fulfillment that began with the divided tongues of fire on the Day of Pentecost.

Note carefully that John's prophecy pointed to the distinguishing feature of the Christ. Fire. Fire fell on the Day of Pentecost. It was a fulfillment of the prophecy. But was that all? Was it just for the 120? Just them? Was it over and done with then? Was it a personal enduement of power that they needed but we don't? Were they the chosen few, and nobody else would ever be given the same wonderful gift? How would that fulfill the prophecy of John? For that matter, how would it fulfill a lot more prophecies about the coming invasion of the Spirit into this world?

There is only one true fulfillment, and it is for God to pour out His Spirit on *all* flesh, soaking us all with the early and latter rain, the golden rain of the fire of heaven.

Let the fires burn! Let the churches blaze! Let the people be like Samson's foxes taking torches into devil's territory. Let those dark places be burnt to ashes by the glory of God!

CHRIST FOR ALL NATIONS CAMPAIGNS: 1975–2012

1975

Gaborone, Botswana

Soweto, South Africa

Cape Town, South Africa

1976

Port Elizabeth, South Africa

Windhoek, Namibia

Manzini, Swaziland

Mbabane, Swaziland

1977

Bushbuckridge, South Africa

Giyani, South Africa

Sibasa, South Africa

Phalaborwa, South Africa

Tzaneen, South Africa

Messina, South Africa

Louis Trichard, South Africa

1978

Seshego, South Africa

Potgietersrus, South Africa

Phalaborwa, South Africa
Njelele, South Africa
Green Valley, South Africa
Qwa-Qwa, South Africa
Bloemfontein, South Africa

1979

Pretoria, South Africa
Malamulele, South Africa
East London, South Africa
Mafikeng, South Africa
Flagstaff, South Africa

1980

Atteridgeville, South Africa
Tembisa, South Africa
Harare, Zimbabwe
Bulawayo, Zimbabwe
Mutare, Zimbabwe

1981

Welkom, South Africa
Soweto, South Africa
Lusaka, Zambia
Kitwe, Zambia
Ndola, Zambia
Kabwe, Zambia
Livingstone, Zambia
Birmingham, England

1982

Newcastle, South Africa

Pietermaritzburg, South Africa

Empangeni, South Africa

Big Bend, Swaziland

Rustenburg, South Africa

Ga-Rankuwa, South Africa

Tlhabane, South Africa

Mabopane, South Africa

Nairobi, Kenya

Ladysmith, South Africa

Cape Town, South Africa

Hammanskraal, South Africa

1983

Perth, Australia

Auckland, New Zealand

Port Elizabeth, South Africa

Dennilton, South Africa

Kwandabele, South Africa

Tafelkop, South Africa

Siyabuswa, South Africa

Helsinki, Finland

Gaborone, Botswana

Francistown, Botswana

Durban, South Africa

Kampala, Uganda

Kwa Thema, South Africa

Trial erection/crusade in the first Big Tent: Mamelodi,
South Africa

1984

Soweto, South Africa
Big Tent dedication: Cape Town, South Africa
Big Tent destroyed: Calcutta, India
Harare, Zimbabwe

1985

Ibadan, Nigeria
Lusaka, Zambia
Lubumbashi, D. R. Congo
Accra, Ghana
Singapore

1986

Kumasi, Ghana
Sekondi Takoradi, Ghana
Harare, Zimbabwe: First Fire Conference & new Big Tent
Blantyre, Malawi
Lagos, Nigeria

1987

Tamale, Ghana
Onitsha, Nigeria
Douala, Cameroon
Mzuzu, Malawi
Singapore
New Orleans, Louisiana, USA

Frankfurt, Germany: Euro-Fire Conference
Ho, Ghana
Cape Coast, Ghana
Dar-es-Salaam, Tanzania
Tema, Ghana

1988

Manila, Philippines
Yaounde, Cameroon
Aba, Nigeria
Nairobi, Kenya
Birmingham, UK: Euro-Fire Conference
Hamburg, Germany
Nakuru, Kenya
Port Harcourt, Nigeria
Kisumu, Kenya
Accra, Ghana

1989

Mombasa, Kenya
Kumba, Cameroon
Enugu, Nigeria
Kampala, Uganda
Riga, USSR
Bukavu, Zaire
Bujumbura, Burundi
Warri, Nigeria
Jos, Nigeria
Kuala Lumpur, Malaysia
Abidjan, Ivory Coast

1990

Meru, Kenya

Machakos, Kenya

Bamenda, Cameroon

Ougadougou, Burkina Faso

Ibadan, Nigeria

Goma, Zaire

Kigali, Rwanda

Butembo, Zaire

Lisbon, Portugal: Euro-Fire Conference

Jinja, Uganda

Kaduna, Nigeria

Ilorin, Nigeria

Cotonou, Benin

1991

Mathare Valley, Kenya

Lome, Togo

Bouake, Ivory Coast

Bobo Dioulasso, Burkina Faso

Jakarta, Indonesia

Kinshasa, Zaire

Kananga, Zaire

Mbuji-Mayi, Zaire

Kisangani, Zaire

Kano, Nigeria

Freetown, Sierra Leone

1992

Mbeya, Tanzania

Bangui, C. A. Republic

Libreville, Gabon

Port Gentil, Gabon

Eldoret, Kenya

Luanda, Angola

Birmingham, UK

Brazzaville, Congo

Kiev, Ukraine

Pointe-Noire, Congo

Conakry, Guinea

Buenos Aires, Argentina

Douala, Cameroon

1993

Dar-es-Salaam, Tanzania

Kumasi, Ghana

Surabaya, Indonesia

Tanga, Tanzania

Maputo, Mozambique

Beira, Mozambique

Odessa, Ukraine

Bamako, Mali

Kingston, Jamaica

Ouagadougou, Burk. Faso

1994

Kibera, Kenya

Madras, India

United Kingdom & Eire: *From Minus to Plus* booklet
distribution

Senajuki, Finland

Lubumbashi, Zaire

Port of Spain, Trinidad

Belo Horizonte, Brazil

Antananarivo, Madagascar

Tarmatave, Madagascar

N'Djamena, Chad

Porto Alegre, Brazil

Sarh, Chad

1995

Porto Novo, Benin

Awasa, Ethiopia

Hyderabad, India

Addis Ababa, Ethiopia

Likasi, Zaire

Kolwezi, Zaire

German-speaking Europe: *From Minus to Plus* booklet
distribution

Cairo, Egypt

Dakar, Senegal

Jakarta, Indonesia

Bamako, Mali

Bissau, Guinea-Bissau

1996

Kara, Togo

Mwanza, Tanzania

Bangalore, India

Medan, Indonesia

Temirtau, Kazakstan

Karabolta, Kyrgyzstan

Arusha, Tanzania

Mombasa, Kenya

Surre Kundra, Gambia

Madurai, India

Hong Kong: *From Minus to Plus* booklet distribution

Parakou, Benin

1997

Yaounde, Cameroon

Colombo, Sri Lanka

Thika, Kenya

Scandinavia: *From Minus to Plus* booklet distribution

Blantyre, Malawi

Lilongwe, Malawi

Ndola, Zambia

Dodoma, Tanzania

Maroua, Cameroon

Pune, India

1998

Bata, Equatorial Guinea

New Delhi, India

Tema, Ghana
Cape Town, South Africa
Dar-es-Salaam, Tanzania
Antananarivo, Madagascar
Freetown, Sierra Leone
Cochin, India
Monrovia, Liberia

1999

Cotonou, Benin
Sekondi Takoradi, Ghana
Cebu City, Philippines
Manila, Philippines
General Santos, Philippines
Böblingen, Germany: Fire Conference
Kigali, Rwanda
Nakuru, Kenya
Moshi, Tanzania
Sicily, Italy
Benin City, Nigeria
Visakapatnum, India

2000

Calabar, Nigeria
Aba, Nigeria
Shillong, India
Khartoum, Sudan
Jimma, Ethiopia
Nazareth, Ethiopia

Moscow, Russia
Lagos, Nigeria
Enugu, Nigeria
Ontario, Canada
Birmingham, UK

2001

Uyo, Nigeria
Onitsha, Nigeria
Owerri, Nigeria
Kinshasa, Rep. of Congo
Ibadan, Nigeria
Oshogbo, Nigeria
Belfast, Ireland
Munich, Germany

2002

Abeokuta, Nigeria
Akure, Nigeria
Ilesa, Nigeria
Kisumu, Kenya
Ogbomosho, Nigeria
Ile-Ife, Nigeria
Singapore, Indonesia

2003

Ado Ekiti, Nigeria
Ondo Town, Nigeria
Makurdi, Nigeria

Owo, Nigeria
Oyo, Nigeria
Okene, Nigeria
Ikare Akoko, Nigeria
Berlin, Germany
Viti Levu, Figi
Ikirun, Nigeria
Warri, Nigeria

2004

Port Harcourt, Nigeria
Ijebu Ode, Nigeria
Shaki, Nigeria
Orlu, Nigeria
Ilorin, Nigeria
Umuahia, Nigeria
Benin City, Nigeria
Calabar, Nigeria

2005

Jos, Nigeria
Aarau, Switzerland
Jalingo, Nigeria
Ayangba, Nigeria
Gboko, Nigeria
Port Moresby, Papua New Guinea
Uromi, Nigeria

2006

Ogoja, Nigeria

Abuja, Nigeria

Juba, Sudan

Wukari, Nigeria

Timisoara, Romania

Lagos, Nigeria

Ikom, Nigeria

2007

Ado Ekiti, Nigeria

Oshogbo, Nigeria

Aba, Nigeria

Kabba, Nigeria

Agbor, Nigeria

Abakaliki, Nigeria

2008

Yola, Nigeria

Awka, Nigeria

Kochi , India

Kafanchan, Nigeria

Nsukka, Nigeria

Ikot Ekpene, Nigeria

Okitipupa, Nigeria

2009

Oleh/Ozoro, Nigeria

Mubi, Nigeria

Bali, Nigeria
Otukpo, Nigeria
Afikpo, Nigeria
Ibadan, Nigeria
Sapele, Nigeria

2010

Ugep, Nigeria
Numan, Nigeria
Takum, Nigeria
Karu, Nigeria
Akure, Nigeria
Ogbomosho, Nigeria
Asaba, Nigeria

2011

Lojoja, Nigeria
Lome, Togo
Okigwe, Nigeria
Zaki Biam, Nigeria
Agbani, Nigeria
Ughelli, Nigeria

2012

Ouagadougou, Burkina Faso
Monrovia, Liberia

NOTES

CHAPTER 1
THREE PILLARS OF WISDOM

1. "There Is Power in the Blood" by Lewis E. Jones. Public domain.

2. George Lindbeck, *The Nature of Doctrine* (Louisville, KY: Westminster John Knox Press, 1984), 117.

CHAPTER 2
GOD HAS TAKEN THE FIELD

1. Arnold Toynbee, *A Study of History*, as quoted in Ronald W. Foulkes, *The Flame Shall Not Be Quenched* (n.p.: Methodist Charismatic Fellowship, 1972), 100.

2. Foulkes, *The Flame Shall Not Be Quenched*.

3. John Wesley, *Explanatory Notes Upon the New Testament* (n.p.: Forgotten Books, 2010), 278.

4. As quoted in Cecil M. Robeck, *Charismatic Experiences in History* (Peabody, MA: Hendrickson Publishers, 1985), 70.

5. John Wesley, "Conversation With the Bishop of Bristol," in *The Works of the Reverend John Wesley, A.M.*, vol. 7 (New York: J. Emory and B. Waugh, 1831), 479; digitalized by Google and available at http://books.google.com.

6. Foulkes, *The Flame Shall Not Be Quenched*.

7. John Wesley, *The Journal of the Rev. John Wesley A.M.*, vol 2, from November 25, 1746 to May 5, 1760 (London: J. Kershaw, 1827), 21; digitalized by Google and available at http://books.google.com.

8. Luke Tyerman, *The Life and Times of the Rev. John Wesley, M.A., Founder of the Methodists*, vol. 1 (London: Hodder and Stoughton, 1870), 229; digitalized by Google and available at http://books.google.com.

9. William Shakespeare, *The Merchant of Venice* 1.1. References are to act and scene.

10. Historical baptismal liturgies invariably show that the chrism of anointing with oil for the reception of the Spirit did not take place until after baptism, signifying the washing away of sins and the candidate becoming regenerate; that is postconversion. See Harold Hunter, *Spirit Baptism: A Pentecostal Alternative* (Lanham, MD: University Press of America, 2009).

11. D. Martyn Lloyd-Jones, *Joy Unspeakable* (Wheaton, IL: Harold Shaw, 1985).

12. This quote by Smith Wigglesworth can be seen in various websites on the Internet.

CHAPTER 3
THE ANOINTING

1. Donald Guthrie, ed., *New Bible Commentary* (Grand Rapids, MI: Wm. B. Eerdmans, 1950), s.v. "ointment."

2. Examples of initial reactions to the tongues phenomenon can be found in F. W. Pitt, *The Tongues Baptism*, and G. H. Lang, *The Early Years of the Tongues Movement*.

3. "My Song Is Love Unknown" by Samuel Crossman. Public domain.

CHAPTER 4
HOW THE GIFTS CAME

1. "Jesus! The Name High Over All" by Charles Wesley. Public domain.

CHAPTER 5
GOLDEN RULES OF THE GIFTS

1. "Souls of Men, Why Will Ye Scatter" by Frederick W. Faber. Public domain.

2. Siegfried Schatzmann, "A Pauline Theology of Charismata" (PhD dissertation, Elim Bible College, Nantwich, UK, n.d.).

3. Elizabeth Stuart, "Love is…Paul," *Expository Times* 102, no. 9: 264–266.

CHAPTER 7
A WORD OF WISDOM

1. William L. Holladay, ed., *A Concise Hebrew and Aramaic Lexicon of the Old Testament* (Grand Rapids, MI: William B. Eerdmans Publishing Company, 1988), 76.

CHAPTER 8
A WORD OF KNOWLEDGE

1. Philip Schaff, ed., *ANF08. The Twelve Patriarchs, Excerpts and Epistles, The Clementia, Apocrypha, Decretals, Memoirs of Edessa and Syriac Documents, Remains of the First,* chapter 37, "Whom to Know Is Life Eternal," Christian Classics Ethereal Library, http://www.ccel.org/ccel/schaff/anf08.vi.iv.vi.xxxvii.html (accessed December 20, 2011).

2. William S. Gilbert, *The Gondoliers*, in William S. Gilbert and Arthur Sullivan, *The Works of Sir William Gilbert and Sir Arthur Sullivan* (n.p.: Kessinger Publishing, 2005), 204.

CHAPTER 9
FAITH

1. William Wordsworth, *The Excursion*, Book Fourth, lines 1293–1295.

2. "Father of Jesus Christ, My Lord" by Charles Wesley. Public domain.

CHAPTER 11
HEALING, PART 2

1. J. B. S. Haldane, *Possible Worlds* (n.p.: Chatto and Windus, 1927), as quoted in Goodreads.com, "Possible Worlds Quotes," http://www.goodreads.com/work/quotes/998920 (accessed January 4, 2012).

CHAPTER 12
MIRACLES

1. George Wigram and Ralph Winter, eds., *Word Study Concordance* (Wheaton, IL: Tyndale House Publishers, 1979), s.v. "miracle."

2. "There's Power in the Blood" by Lewis E. Jones. Public domain.

CHAPTER 13
PROPHECY

1. James Dunn, *Jesus and the Spirit* (Belleville, MI: Westminster/John Knox Press, 1979).

2. R. P. Spittler, "Glossolalia," in Stanley Burgess, Gary McGee and Patrick Alexander, eds., *Dictionary of Pentecostal and Charismatic Movements* (Grand Rapids, MI: Zondervan Publishing House, 1988), 336.

CHAPTER 14
DISCERNMENT

1. Ralph P. Martin, *The Spirit and the Congregation* (Grand Rapids, MI: William B. Eerdmans Publishing Company, 1984), 14.

CHAPTER 15
TONGUES AND INTERPRETATION

1. *Die Berliner Erklärung* was issued in 1909 by fifty-six evangelical (Pietist-Holiness) leaders following serious mishaps and mishandling of initial Pentecostal meetings

in Germany. It had a traumatic and deadening effect upon reception of the Pentecostal movement among evangelicals in Germany. Only some eighty years later was a softening of this attitude being seen, particularly to Reinhard Bonnke.

CHAPTER 16
DIVIDED TONGUES AS OF FIRE

1. Critical methods that address the issues of who had written what and when are basically in error. The approach to Scripture has to be in faith. The battle between the two standpoints is still going on today. The Pentecostal movement used to be despised because, it was claimed, it produced no theology and no theologians. The argument is somewhat faulty. Pentecost is plain enough in Scripture, and theologians ought to have produced a true theology of the Holy Spirit long before Pentecostals ever existed. The trouble is that the pre-Pentecostal movement theologians should have provided us with the theology, but they had none. There was no serious theology of the Ascension or of the Holy Spirit. Instead of complaining that there was no Pentecostal theology, perhaps they should have asked themselves why. Fortunately there are now Spirit-baptised scholars with insight and well-established academic credentials occupying prominent niches in the architecture of the church. Hopefully the balance is being redressed—on both sides.

2. This is a statement of the general Christian experience, not a doctrinal statement about the baptism in the Spirit.

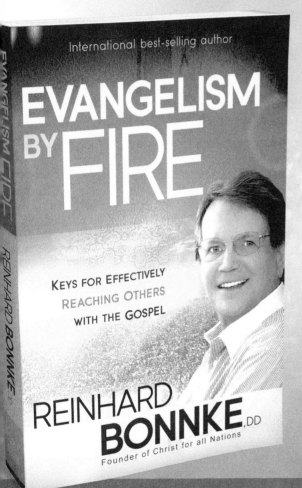

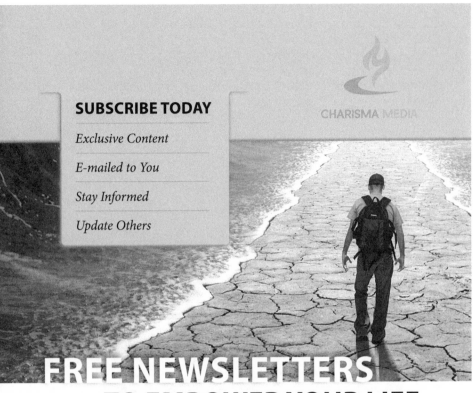